THE
BEGINNERCLASSICAL
GUITARMETHOD

Master classical guitar technique, repertoire and musicality

ROSS**TROTTIER**

The Beginner Classical Guitar Method

Published by **www.fundamental-changes.com**

ISBN: 978-1-911267-81-2

www.fundamental-changes.com

Twitter: **@guitar_joseph**

Over 10,000 fans on Facebook: **FundamentalChangesInGuitar**

Instagram: **FundamentalChanges**

For over 250 Free Guitar Lessons with Videos Check Out

www.fundamental-changes.com

Contents

Introduction

Classical guitar is an incredibly fulfilling, in-depth style of music. The amount of repertoire available to the instrument is vast, spanning hundreds of years. This book will teach you to play classical guitar by integrating practical examples and real-world examples. When working through the material, be sure not to skip any steps or pages. Each example and piece of repertoire is designed to build upon the last, and is sure to make your introduction to the instrument painless as well as fun.

Before any playing can be done, there are a few things every student must understand. First, a few golden rules about the guitar itself must be grasped. Second, basic technical principles must be observed *from day one*. Hours, months and even years of frustration can be avoided by understanding some basic information.

Get the Audio

The audio files for this book are available to download for free from **www.fundamental-changes.com** and the link is in the top right corner. Simply select this book title from the drop-down menu and follow the instructions to get the audio.

We recommend that you download the files directly to your computer, not to your tablet, and extract them there before adding them to your media library. You can then put them on your tablet, iPod or burn them to CD. On the download page there is a help PDF and we also provide technical support via the contact form.

Kindle / eReaders

To get the most out of this book, remember that you can double tap any image to enlarge it. Turn off 'column viewing' and hold your kindle in landscape mode.

For over 250 Free Guitar Lessons with Videos Check out:

www.fundamental-changes.com

Twitter: @guitar_joseph

FaceBook: FundamentalChangesInGuitar

Instagram: FundamentalChanges

Golden Rule #1: When fretting notes, the strings are pressed to the *frets*, not the fretboard

I remember the day that this piece of information was revealed to me. I was already attending university for classical guitar, and it continues to boggle my mind why *nobody told me*. My professor, Jonathan Leathewood, mentioned this principle casually. Nobody in the class believed Jonathan at first, but when we checked for ourselves we were shocked.

The string is pressed to the fret, not the fretboard. The photo below illustrates this. Notice the gap between the string and the fretboard itself.

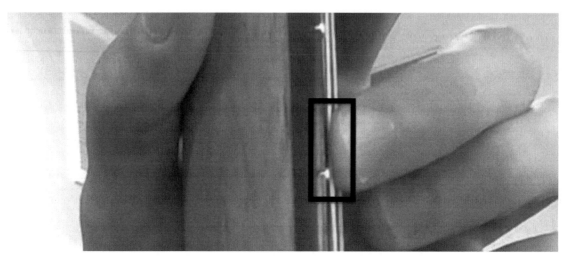

This is an extremely important observation to make from the start. It takes almost no pressure to get a good note to come out of a classical guitar. Many students apply far too much pressure because they are not paying attention to finger placement. Buzzy notes ensue and, generally, the first reflex is to add more pressure. This causes physical pain and limits the mobility of your hand.

If, on the other hand, you firmly press the string to the fret, the ease of play is considerable. Pressing the string to the fret requires the finger tip to be as close to the fret as possible without spilling over it. Also, it is important to angle your fingers slightly towards the fret. It is also of upmost importance that you are using the tip of your finger.

Never play classical guitar with the pads of your fingers!

Golden Rule #2: To achieve the best tone, push the strings into motion rather than striking them

Here is a cool piece of information: the sound produced by classical guitars does not come from the hole.

The sound comes from the top of the guitar, not the sound hole. When the string is attacked, it vibrates the top of the guitar. The sound hole acts as a resonator, but is not the primary sound delivery mechanism. This observation is incredibly important, because it will have an enormous effect on your tone as well as volume.

The string, when plucked, should be plucked in such a way that it is pushed towards the top until the string releases off the finger-tip. Therefore, plucking is a movement which moves the string inwards towards the top, not straight up and down. Volume and roundness of tone will increase dramatically when observing this principle.

Basic Guitar Technique

When sitting with your guitar, one foot must be elevated to raise the headstock to a playable level. Plant both feet and place the guitar's hips between your legs.

Your fretting hand must follow a few basic principles. Squeezing is not necessary most of the time. Finger pressure comes from pulling lightly with your entire arm. Your finger tips should touch the strings, your thumb should touch the back of the neck, and the rest of your hand cannot touch the guitar at all. Do not grasp the neck as if you are picking something up.

To find the best position for your plucking hand, first hold your hand out directly in front of you. Next, make sure your wrist is straight and allow your fingers to dangle limply.

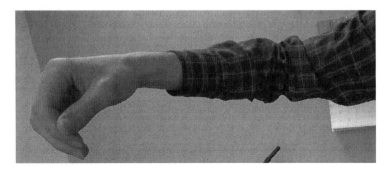

Next, move your right hand and lightly rest your thumb on the A-string. Observe the triangle shape created with the thumb, fingers and strings. Your thumb should never be on the inside of your hand.

Regarding Practice

Learning to practise well is essential to your success. Practice must be done regularly and it must be focused. Structured practice includes sight reading, examples and repertoire. This book focuses on repertoire. Time should be taken to learn the fundamentals of music itself. This includes reading music, music theory and the rudiments of rhythm. Also, practise slowly and WITH A METRONOME.

It is unlike me to use all caps. Therefore, understand the importance of a metronome!

Chapter One – Basic Technique, Warm-ups and Melodies

Example 1a is the most important warm-up example in this entire book. It is foundational and should be done every single day at the start of practice. When plucking the strings, the motion should start from the big knuckle at the base of your finger. The smaller knuckles do not engage the string, but bend as a part of the follow-through of the stroke.

This example should be done with free stroke as well as rest stroke. *Free stroke* is done by plucking the string while the finger misses the adjacent strings. *Rest stroke* is done by plucking directly through the string, stopping on the adjacent string. With each stroke, remember to totally relax your finger after the movement has been executed.

Free Stroke

Rest Stroke

Each finger should be used individually for this example. First, your index finger, which is represented in this book with the letter *i*. Next, your middle finger, represented with the letter *m*. Then your annular finger (ring finger), represented with the letter *a*. Finally, your thumb, which is represented with the letter *p*.

Notice the dark line with the double dots at the end of the second to last measure. This instructs the player to repeat the section. After the section is played for the second time, the player moves along to the end.

Example 1a

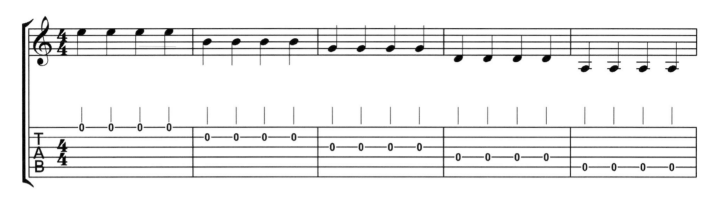

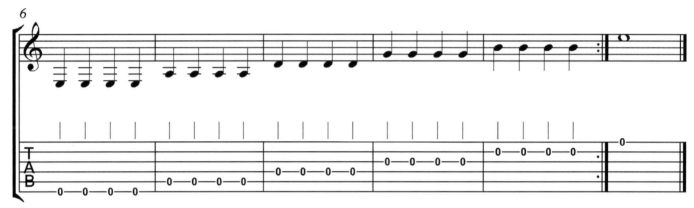

Example 1b introduces alternation between thumb and fingers. This example should utilize free stroke as well as rest stroke with the fingers. Notice the picking pattern above the notes, listing the right-hand fingers. The example lists the pattern p then i. This instructs you to use your thumb, then your index. Notice the word "simile" after the pattern. Simile means to maintain the pattern throughout the example, or until otherwise noted. This example should also use the pattern thumb then middle (p, m) as well as thumb then annular (p, a).

Example 1b

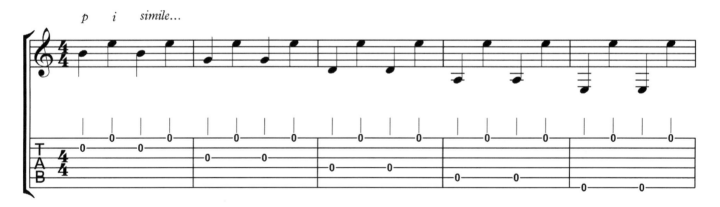

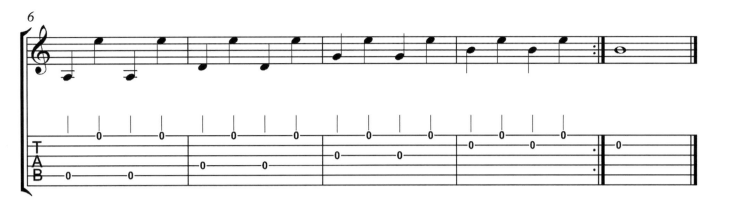

Example 1c introduces a fingerpicking pattern that requires three fingers instead of two. In this example the thumb, index and middle fingers are used. Notice that the last measure consists of the B-string as a whole-note, ringing through the entire measure. Strike this string with either the middle finger or the ring finger.

Example 1c

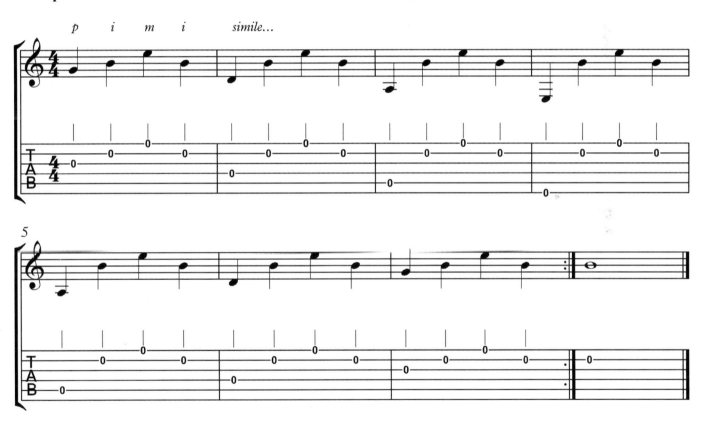

Example 1d introduces another fingerpicking pattern, this time utilizing all four fingers. Notice that the pattern ends with the thumb on the D-string.

Example 1d

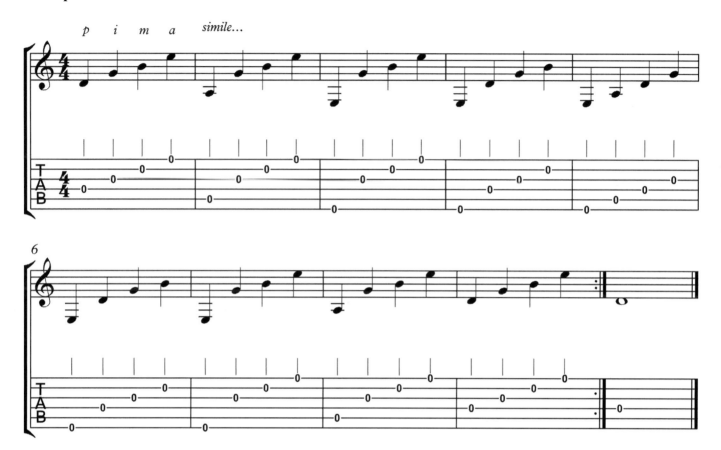

Example 1e introduces the left hand. The left-hand fingers are labelled as follows: 1 = index, 2 = middle, 3 = ring, 4 = pinky. Be careful to switch each finger as needed, not all at once. When switching from the second measure to the third, the index finger can be left in place as an anchor finger between each chord.

Example 1e

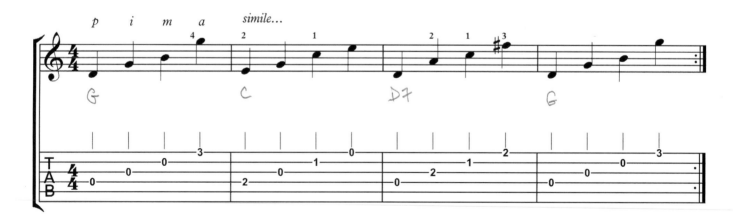

Example 1f uses the same chord progression, but switches the right-hand pattern to a reverse pattern. This new pattern works from the higher strings to the lower strings.

Example 1f

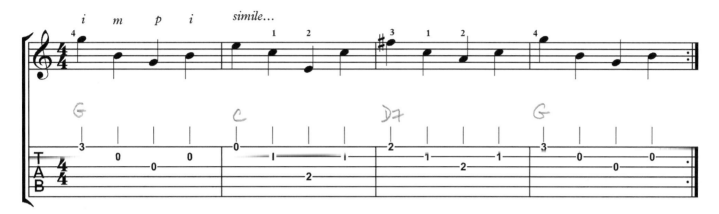

Example 1g introduces you to a pattern where strings are skipped, instead of being played adjacently.

Example 1g

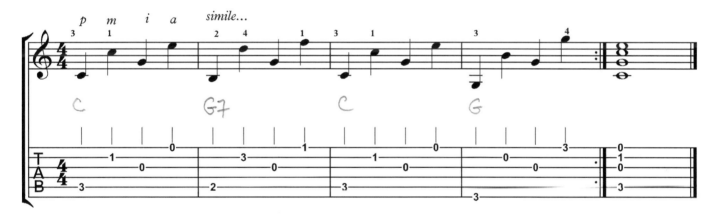

These examples should be practised slowly at first. Many of these concepts and techniques will reappear in this book, and it is of upmost importance that the student takes time to digest these examples. Use them to warm up daily and you will reap massive benefits. Neglect to warm up at your own peril. Each chapter will begin with examples and proceed with melodies, etudes and pieces.

Next, it is time to learn some simple, yet familiar, melodies. Learn each melody below slowly and do your best to follow the fingerings.

Example 1h - Good King Wenceslas

Example 1i - Joy to the World

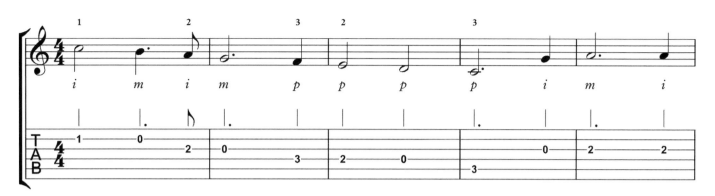

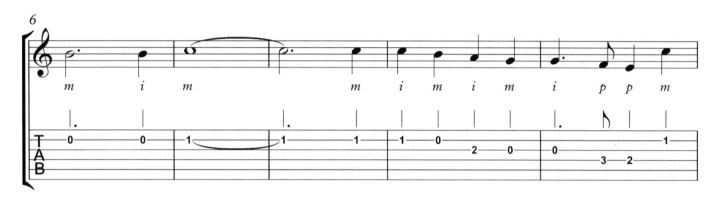

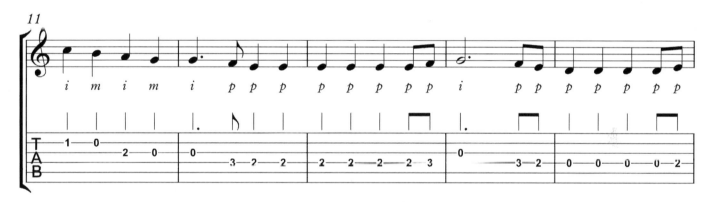

Example 1j - Silent Night

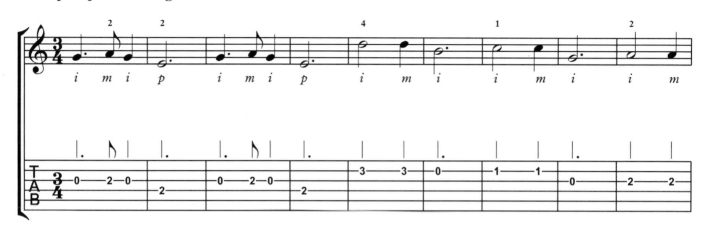

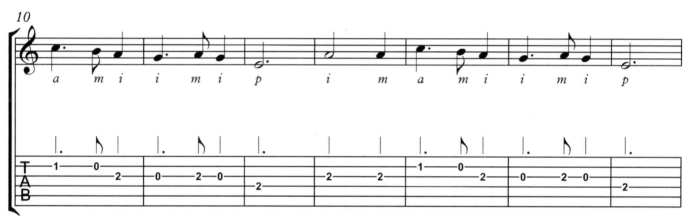

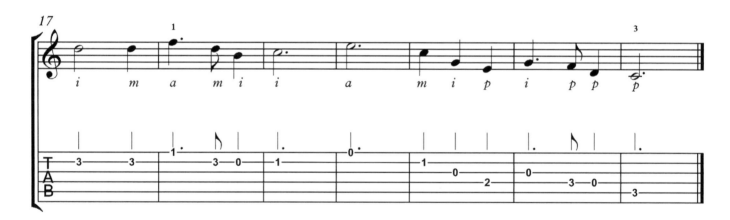

Example 1k - Amazing Grace

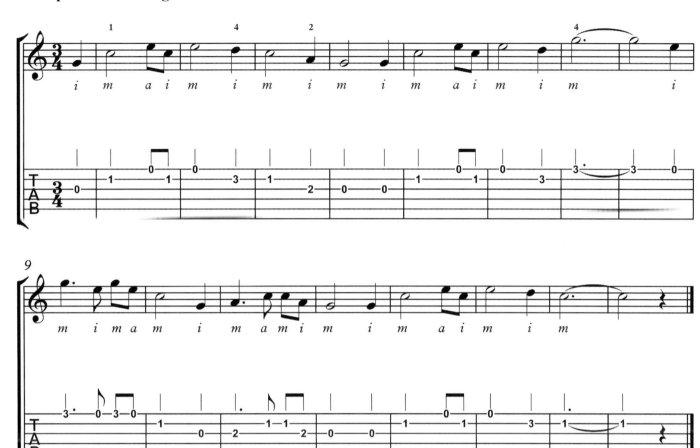

Now it is time to begin working on pieces from the classical guitar repertoire. This chapter concludes with one of classical guitar's most celebrated composers, Fernando Sor. His Opus 60 is renowned for being both deep and suitable for beginners.

Example 1l - Fernando Sor Op. 60 No. 1

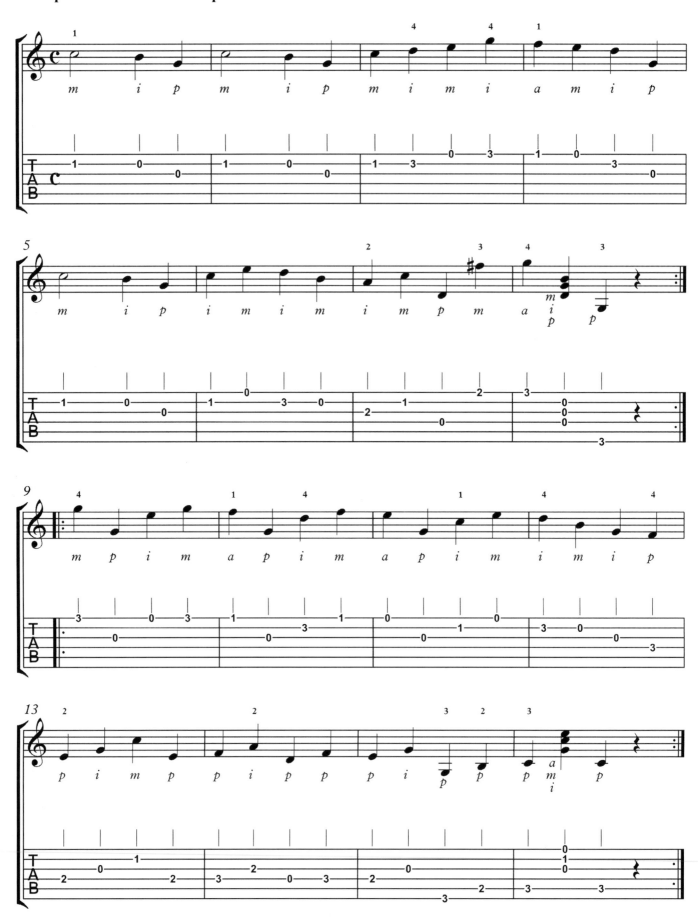

Example 1m - Fernando Sor Op. 60 No. 2

Chapter Two – Introduction to Arpeggios and the Key of C Major

One of the reasons classical guitar sounds so brilliant is the fact that it can arpeggiate across a wide span of musical intervals. This chapter is going to introduce Mauro Giuliani's *120 Right Hand Studies*. These should be used every day to warm up. This book is going to introduce a handful of them each chapter.

These examples use basic C Major and G7 chords to train a huge variety of fingerpicking patterns. Practising these every day will have a huge pay out in terms of technical skill. Notice the fingerings, as well as the marking "simile…".

Example 2a - Mauro Giuliani Op. 1 No. 1

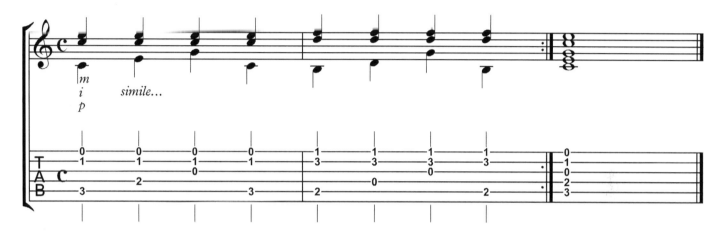

Example 2b - Mauro Giuliani Op. 1 No. 2

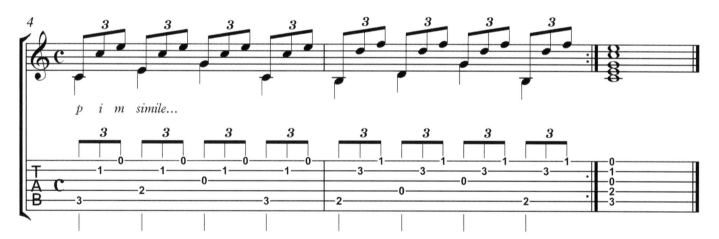

Example 2c - Mauro Giuliani Op. 1 No. 3

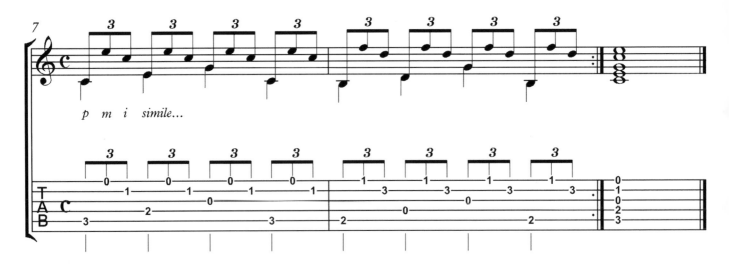

The Key of C Major

Most music is played in a key. A key, in its essence, is a pattern that is centred around one note. Most pieces have a note that feels like *home*. The music then drifts away from that home note, causing tension for the listener. In general, the song drifts back to the home note and completes itself.

In the key of C Major, our home note is C. For the next handful of examples, we will be using the C Major scale.

Example 2d – The C Major Scale

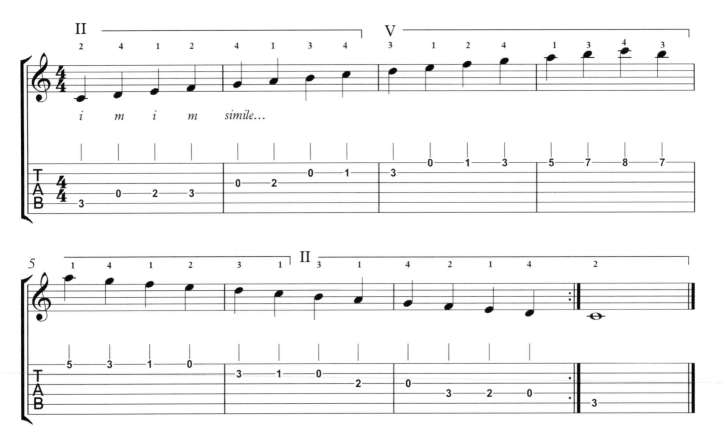

To build chords out of the notes within this scale, pick groups of thirds. Thirds stack up nicely, as shown below. The roman numerals indicate the note in the scale that the chord is built off. The second note of the scale is D, therefore the chord that is based off D is labelled as ii. Lower case indicates Minor chords, upper case indicates Major chords; the degree symbol (°) indicates Diminished chords.

Example 2e – Chords in C-Major

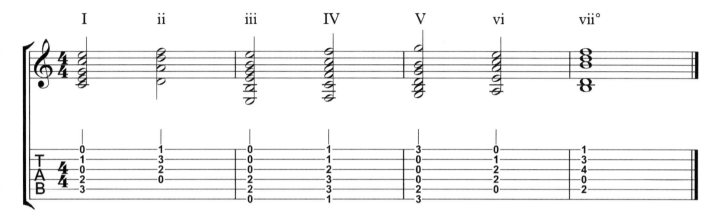

For more scales and chords, please refer to the last chapter of this book.

Mauro Giuliani wrote a large amount of material. This text draws from his Opus 50 – an excellent and pleasant set of etudes. His Op. 50 No. 1 is in the key of C and introduces the idea of double stops – two notes being played simultaneously – and some basic arpeggiation.

When confronted with the double stops, an alternation between (p,i) and (p,m) should be executed. During the arpeggio section, observe the fingerings listed. The pattern will generally use the middle finger on the E-string when played as a double stop. The pattern will also generally use the annular finger on the high E-string when played as a double stop with the thumb.

Example 2f - Mauro Giuliani Op 50 No. 1

Mauro's Op. 50 No. 2 is an exceptional example introducing the concept of balancing multiple melodies at once. The melodies are taken and incorporated with pedal tones in the second half of the study. The sixteenth notes in the last half should be practised very slowly at first and brought up to speed incrementally.

Notice the note at the beginning of the piece. The measure which the note belongs to is only an eighth note in duration. This is called a pickup measure. You begin the piece on the "and" of the two when counting in.

Example 2g - Mauro Giuliani Op 50 No. 2

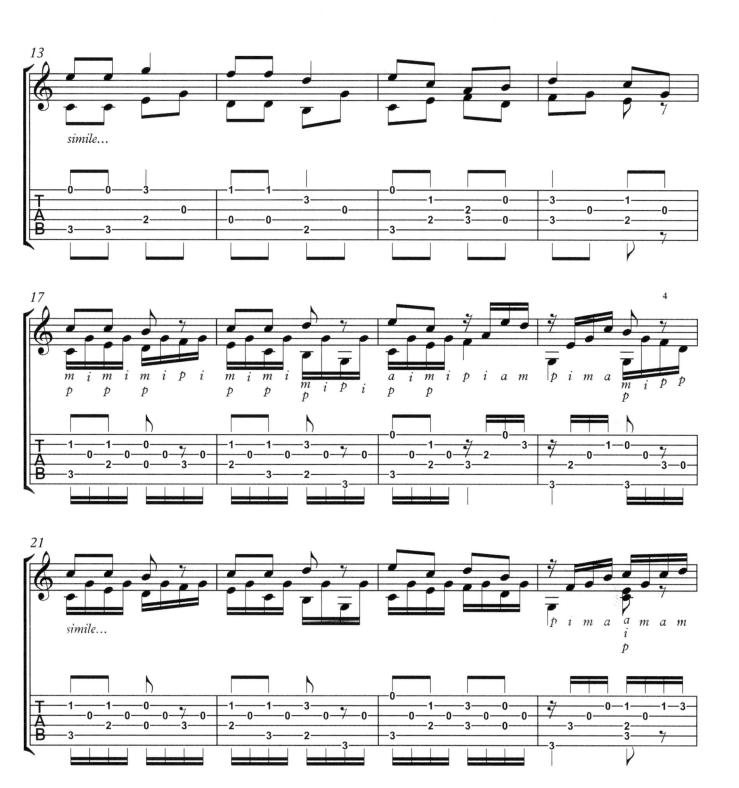

A long-time favorite of budding musicians is Beethoven's *Fur Elise*. Though originally composed for piano, this classic sounds exquisite on guitar. Be careful to follow each finger marking closely, as well as observing the repeated sections.

Also, it is important to note the first and second ending of the first section. The area under the brackets labeled *1.* will be played the first time around. The second time through the section, play the area under the second bracket (marked *2.*) instead of the first.

Notice the measure at the beginning, which lasts only a quarter note. When counting into this piece, start on 3. Make sure to observe the repeats correctly as well, leaving the pickup measure out when taking the repeat.

Example 2h - Beethoven's Fur Elise

Using the thumb for scales is an extremely useful skill. Sor's Op. 60 No. 3 is absolutely perfect for developing this skill. The thumb should be used for almost the entire piece, except for the end where marked. The scales in this piece are played in what is called a "closed position". Open strings will not be used, for the most part.

This etude introduces the overlapping notes of the guitar. Each note on the guitar, save the highest and lowest, can be played in multiple areas on the neck.

Example 2i - Fernando Sor's Op. 60 No. 3

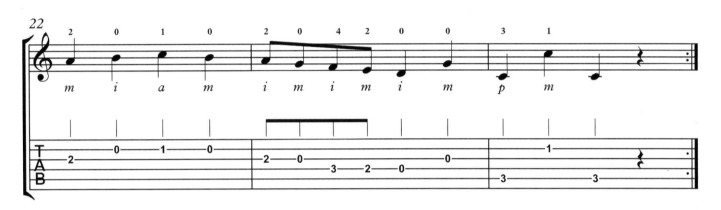

The fourth etude in Fernando Sor's Op. 60 is written in C Minor. The minor scale still centres on C, but uses a different pattern. Be careful to observe the flats on B, E and A. The rhythms are a bit trickier, using dotted eigtht notes as well as sixteenth notes.

Example 2j - Fernando Sor's Op. 60 No. 4

Chapter Three – Mixing Arpeggios and Scales

These next three arpeggio examples are a variation using the same chords from the arpeggios from the last chapter. Notice that the patterns closely mirror each other, but still add variation into the mix.

When improving guitar coordination, variety is equally important to repitition.

Example 3a - Mauro Giuliani Op. 1 No. 4

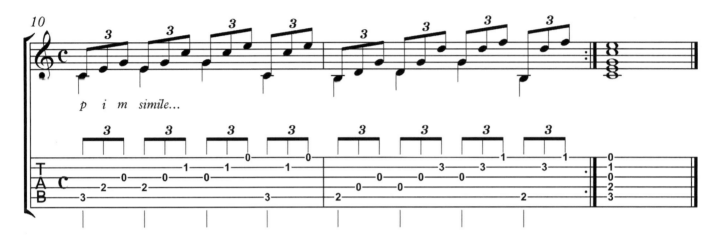

Example 3b - Mauro Giuliani Op. 1 No. 5

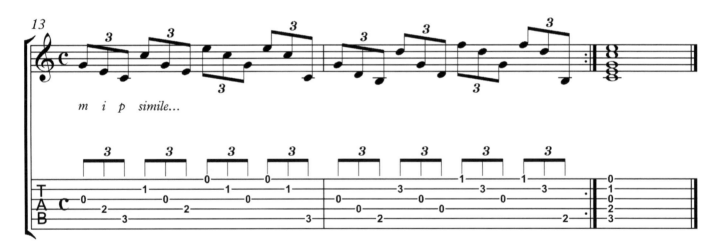

Example 3c - Mauro Giuliani Op. 1 No. 6

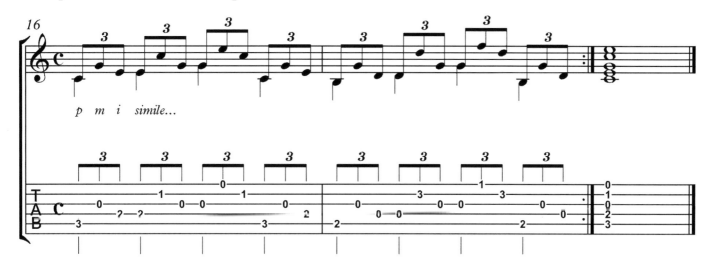

Guiliani's Op 50 No. 3 introduces more variety into the mix. It is in the same key as the first two etudes of the series. This etude, however, mixes triplets with sixteenth notes. Be sure to make the triplets even within the beat, as well as the sixteenth notes.

Example 3d - Mauro Giuliani Op 50 No. 3

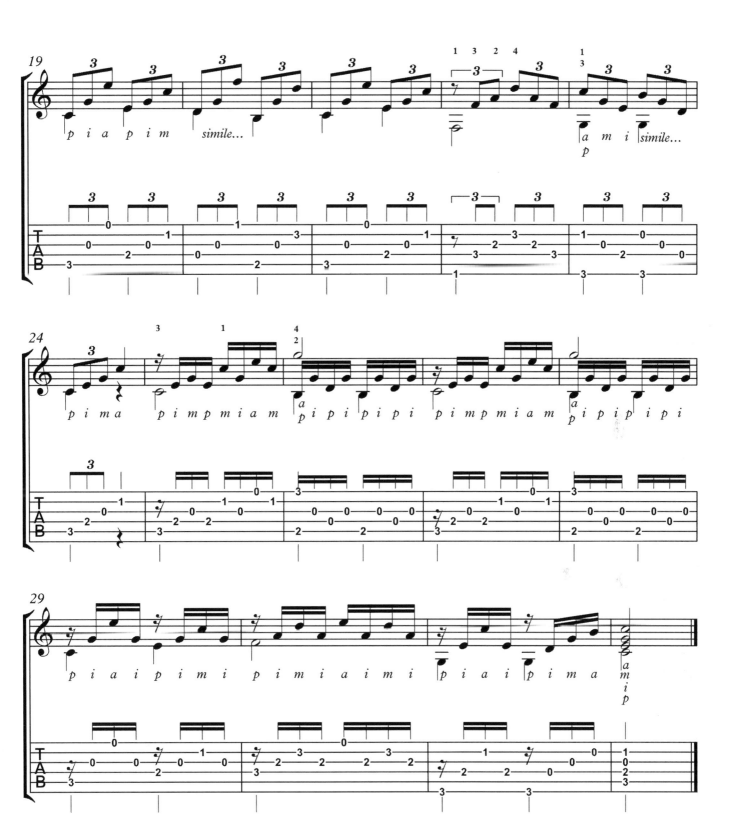

Sor's Op. 60 No. 5 is really excellent for developing scale technique. Starting in A Minor, and eventually moving to A Major, this piece of music is exceedingly lovely. Notice the key signature change halfway through the piece. Use this piece to develop your scales, as well as your ability to play those scales with passion. This etude is begging for some great phrasing.

Also, notice that the time signature is 6/8. Each beat is broken into triplets. At the end, the S symbol indicates that the player should return to the beginning and play to "FINE".

Example 3e - Fernando Sor's Op. 60 No. 4

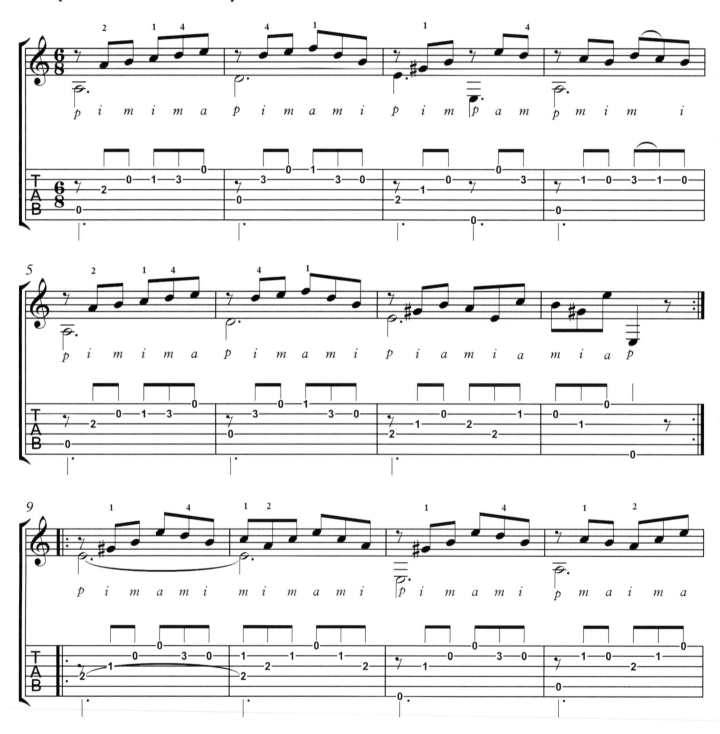

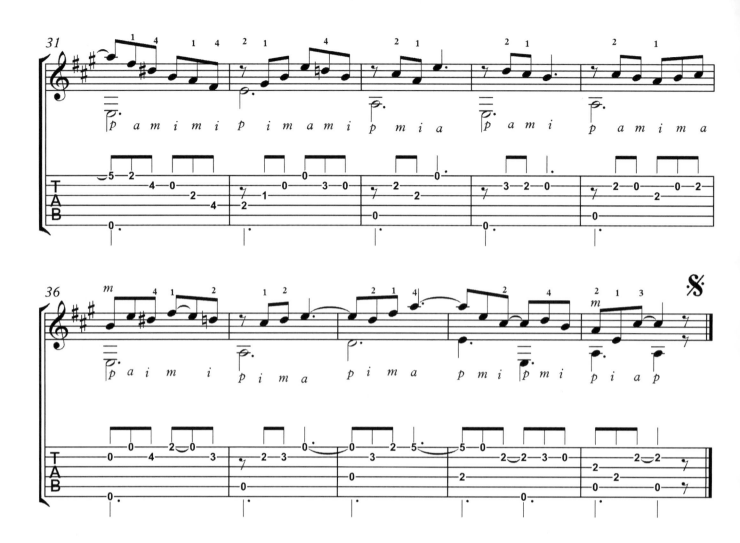

Chapter Four – Thumb Arpeggios and an Introduction to Voice Balancing

The next three arpeggio examples introduce patterns in which strings are skipped.

Example 4a - Mauro Giuliani Op. 1 No. 7

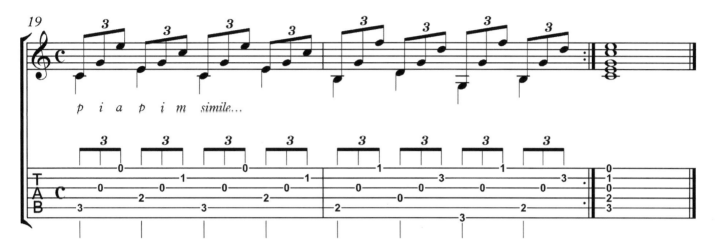

Example 4b - Mauro Giuliani Op. 1 No. 8

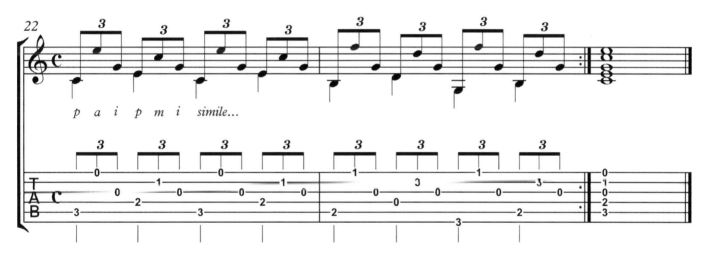

Example 4c - Mauro Giuliani Op. 1 No. 9

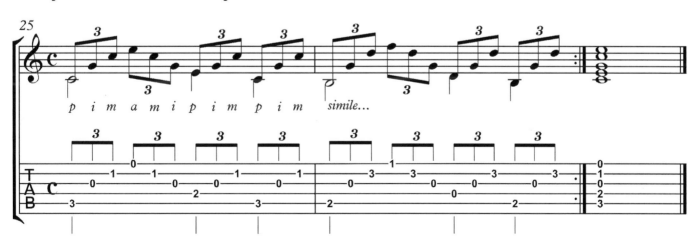

Next, Guiliani is going to illustrate how to play arpeggios with just the thumb, while maintaining a melody with the fingers. This etude is also very beautiful, broken into triplets, and should be practised very slowly. Strive to make the melody sing out above the arpeggios.

Example 4d - Mauro Giuliani Op 50 No. 4

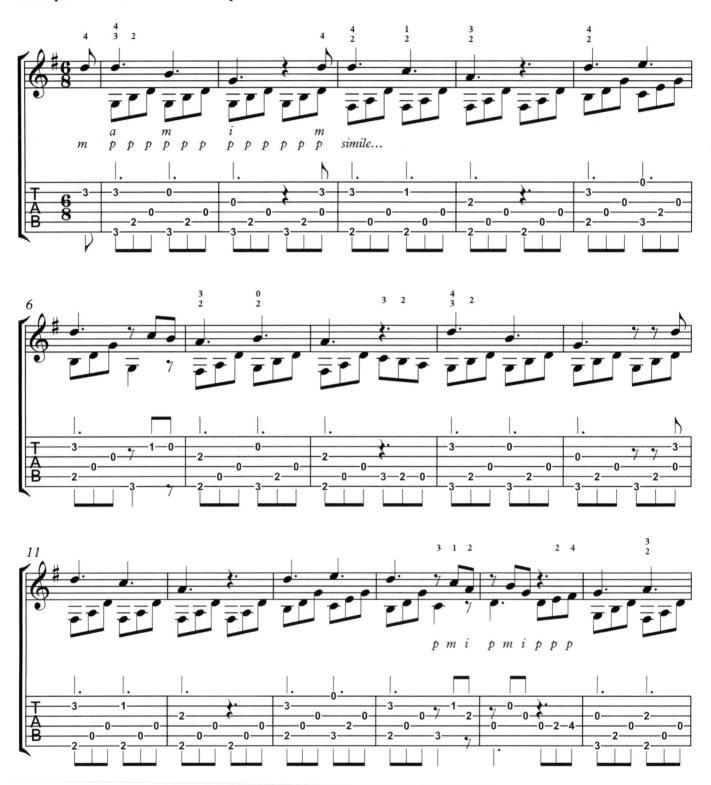

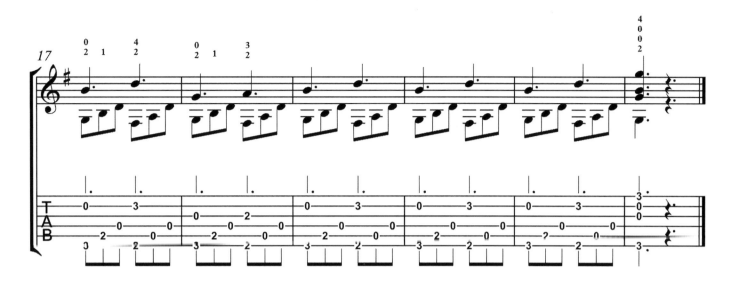

Fernando Sor's Op. 60 No. 6 is another exceedingly lovely example. This etude focuses on mixing apreggiation with scales while balancing multiple voices.

Be sure to follow these fingerings very closely, as the thumb plays a very important role here.

Example 4e - Fernando Sor's Op. 60 No. 6

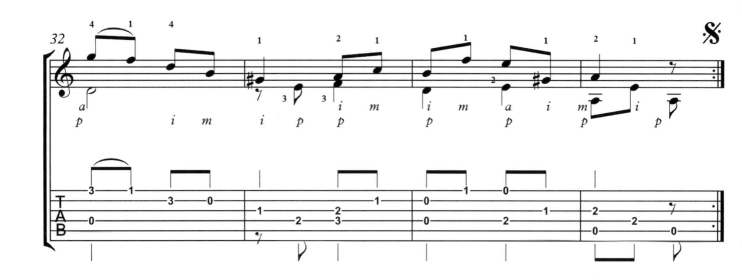

Chapter Five – Parallel Intervals, Advanced Arpeggios and the Barre

The next three arpeggio examples extend the patterns from the last chapter. Each pattern outlines some skipped strings as well as adjacent strings. The last example incorporates rests in a very interesting way. Use your thumb to damp the bass notes when the rests show up.

Example 5a - Mauro Giuliani Op. 1 No. 10

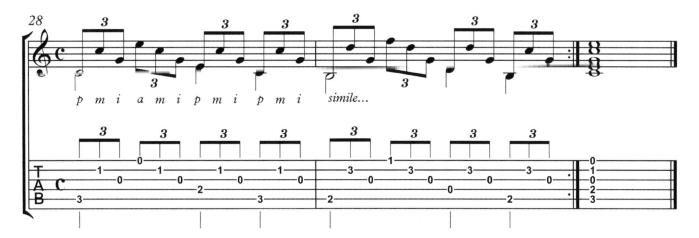

Example 5b - Mauro Giuliani Op. 1 No. 11

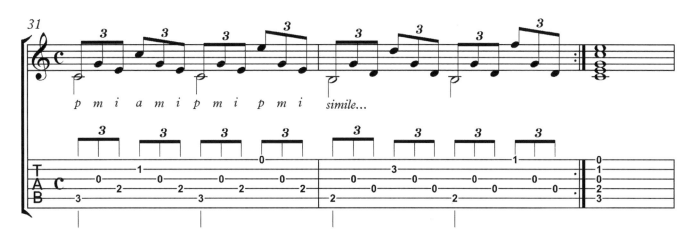

Example 5c - Mauro Giuliani Op. 1 No. 12

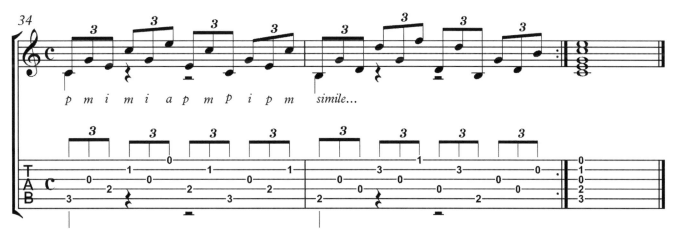

Guiliani's Op. 50 No. 5 is a rapid, yet fun etude. Practise this one extremely slowly at first, and bring it up to speed one step at a time. Paying close attention to the fingerings is an absolute necessity.

Example 5d - Mauro Giuliani Op 50 No. 5

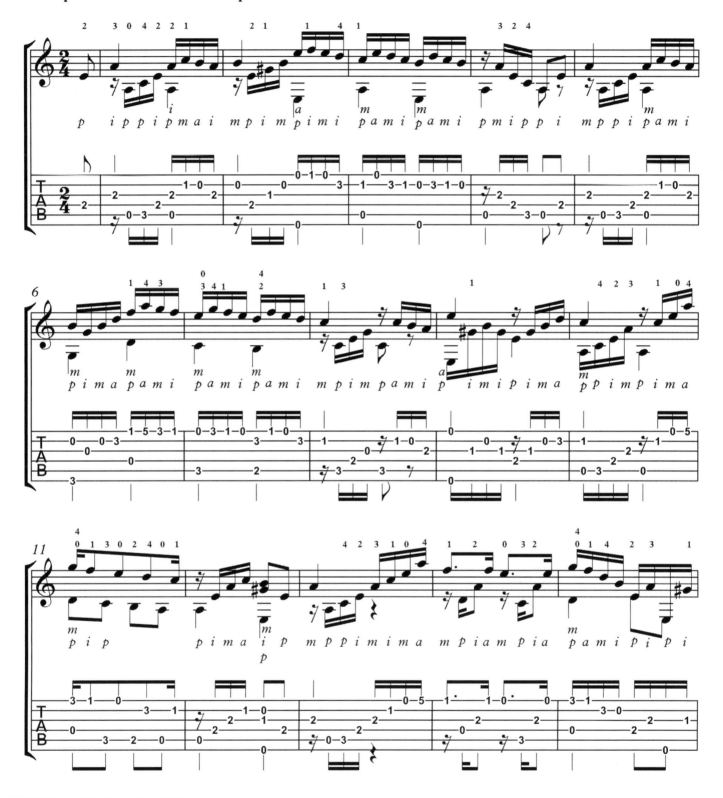

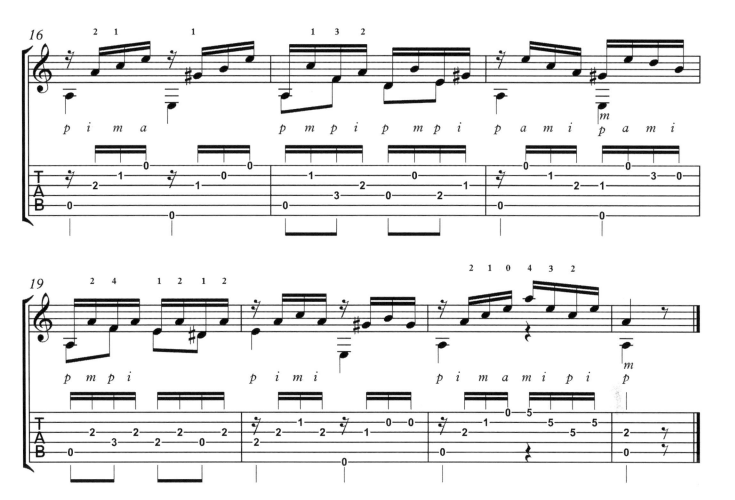

Fernando Sor's Op. 60 No. 13 is a great example for paralell intervals, specifically focusing on thirds and sixths. Almost the entire piece consists of pairs of notes moving in paralell motion.

Be sure to use the thumb for all of the down-stemmed notes.

Example 5e - Fernando Sor's Op. 60 No. 13

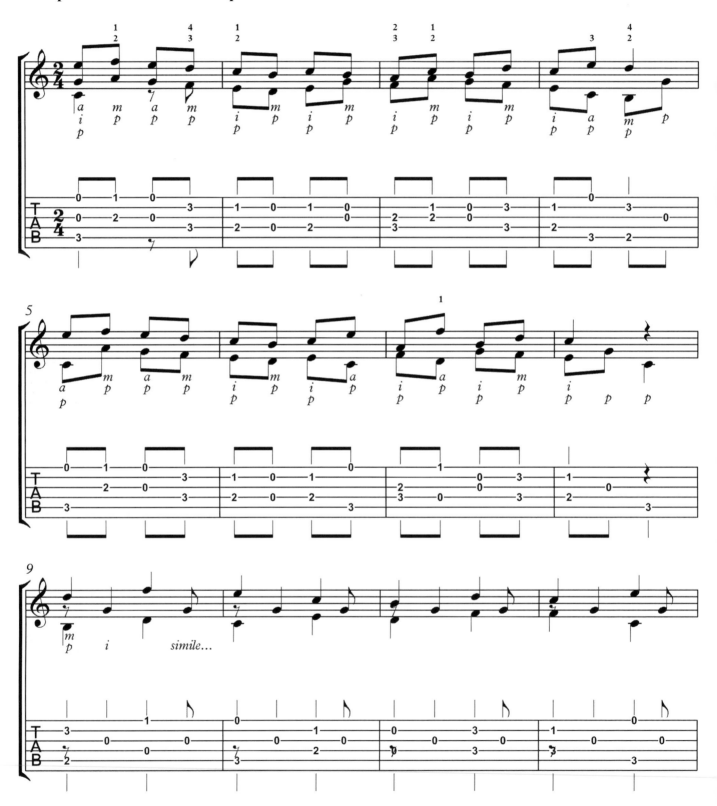

Francisco Tárrega is classical guitar's most celebrated composer for a reason. His music is absolutely beautiful, and has a very nostalgic, romantic sound. His Etude in C will help you devolop your voice-balancing skills. Emphasize the first note of every triplet and play the notes in between a bit quieter. This etude introduces the barre, both full and half. A full barre (C) stops all six strings using the index; a half barre (1/2C) stops only the three highest sounding strings.

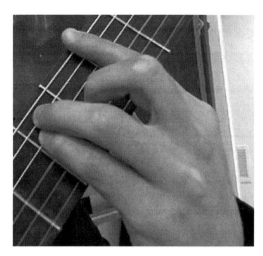

It is extremely important to be sure that your barre is on its side as well as parallel with the fret.

Example 5f - Francisco Tárrega Etude in C

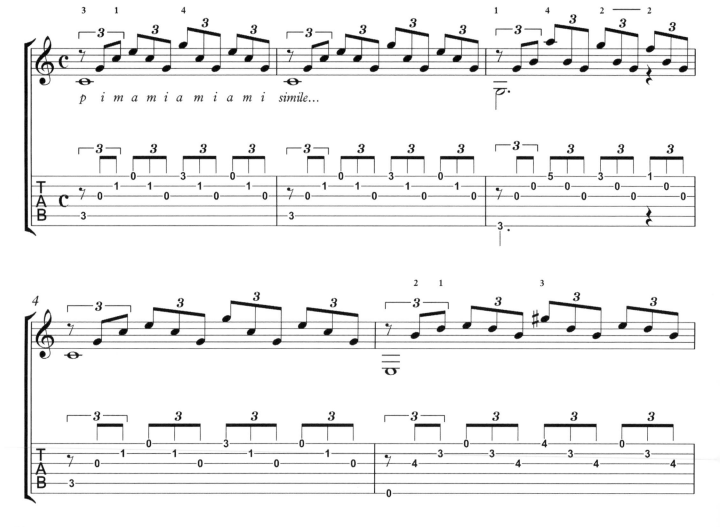

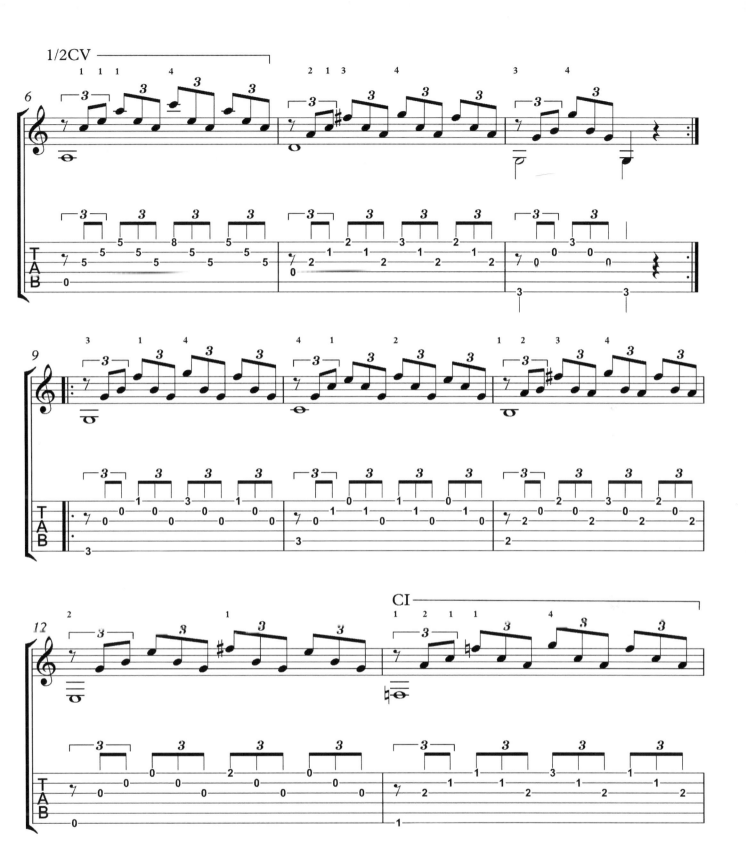

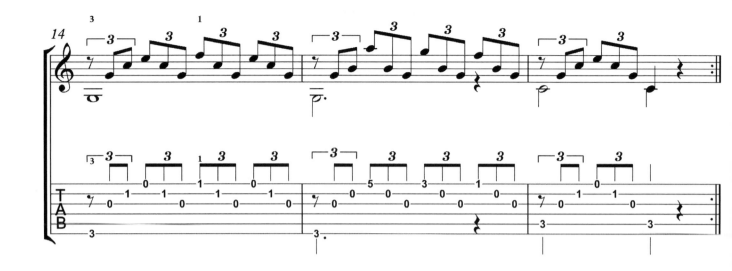

Chapter Six – Grace Notes and Mixing Double Stops with Arpeggios

In the next three arpeggio examples, it is time to begin using two fingers simultaneously. These patterns provide an introduction to this idea, using two fingers at once on each beat.

Example 6a - Mauro Giuliani Op. 1 No. 13

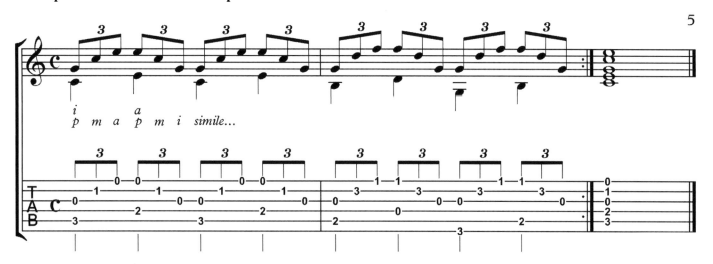

Example 6b - Mauro Giuliani Op. 1 No. 14

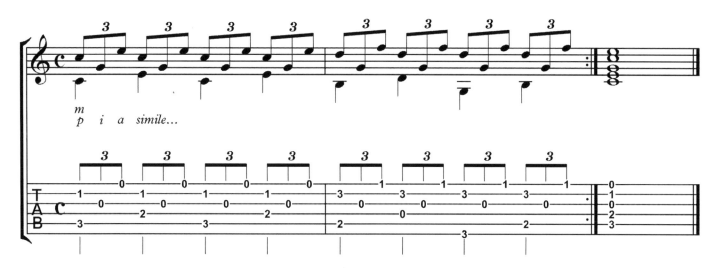

Example 6c - Mauro Giuliani Op. 1 No. 15

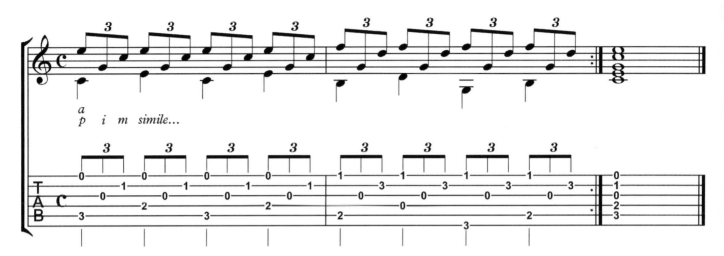

This next etude by Mauro Giuliani is another rapid scale example. This time, however, the use of grace notes is included. To execute a grace note, play the first note and slur to the second immediately. Execute this all on the beat.

Notice the opportunity to use rests in the bass on the third note of each triplet, using the thumb to create a staccato effect.

Example 6d - Mauro Giuliani Op 50 No. 6

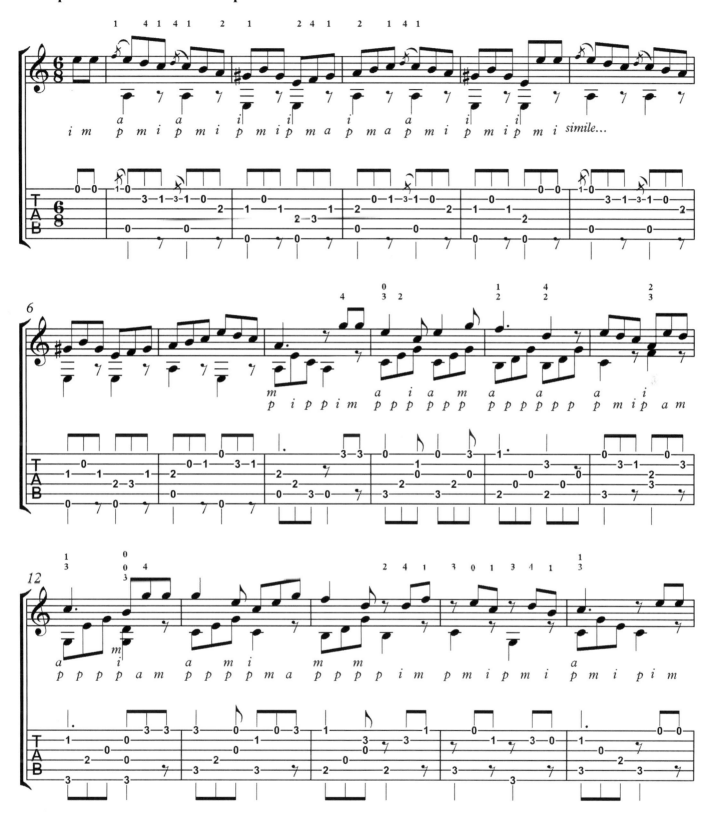

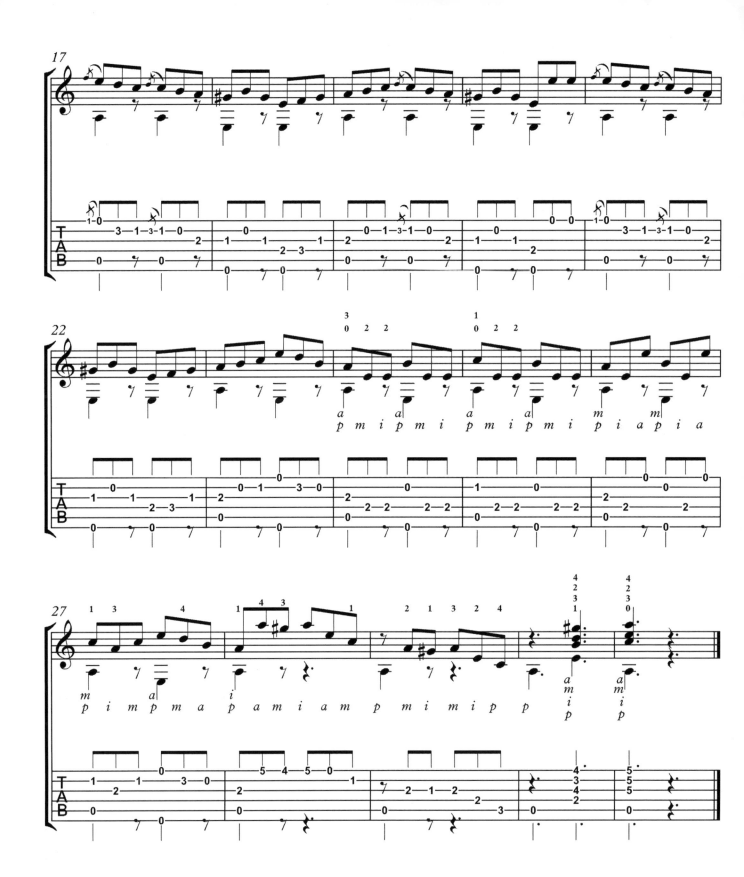

The next etude, another by Fernando Sor, is a bit slower and more melancholy. Be careful to make each chord sound as big as possible, as this piece sounds best when played with a full tone.

It is important to notice the repeats and the first and second endings.

Example 6e - Fernando Sor's Op. 60 No. 14

Chapter Seven – Examples in Speed

The next three arpeggio examples further the technique of using two notes at once, and introduce the idea of using three notes at once.

Example 7a - Mauro Giuliani Op. 1 No. 16

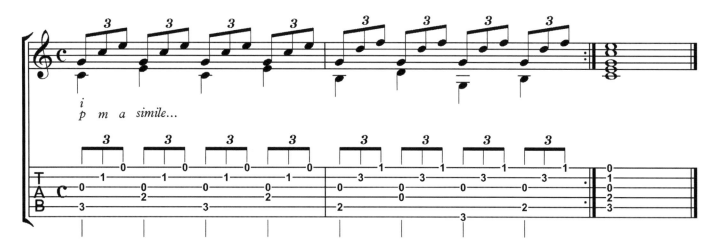

Example 7b - Mauro Giuliani Op. 1 No. 17

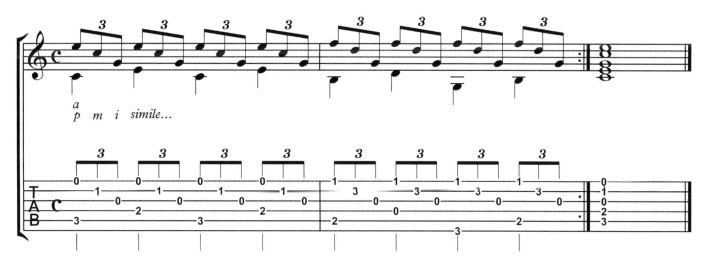

Example 7c - Mauro Giuliani Op. 1 No. 18

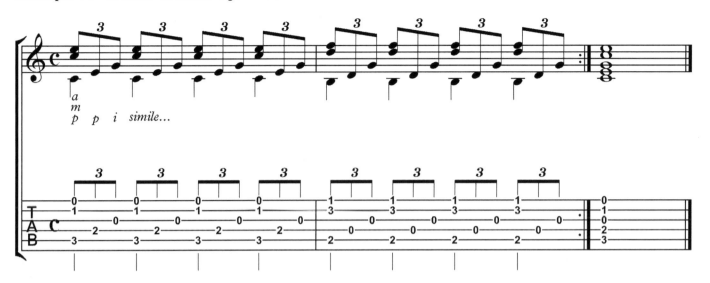

Giuliani is now going to help further the technique of arpeggiation. This etude mixes many of the ideas presented in the etudes from previous chapters and moves at a rapid pace. As with all fast studies, practise this one slowly at first.

Example 7d - Mauro Giuliani Op 50 No. 13

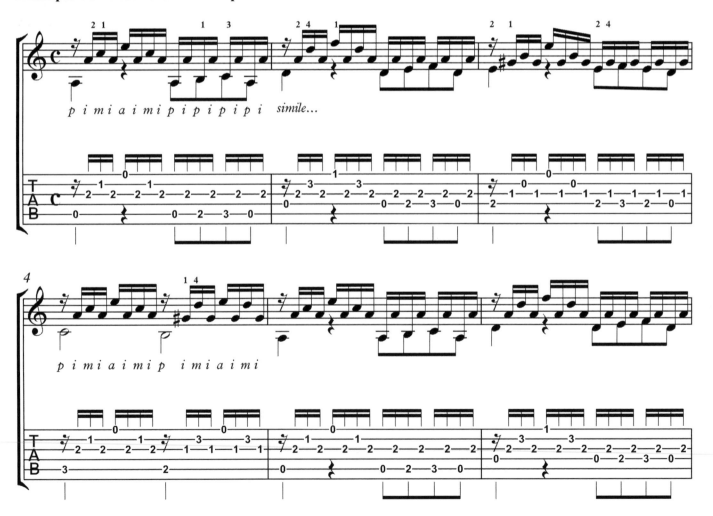

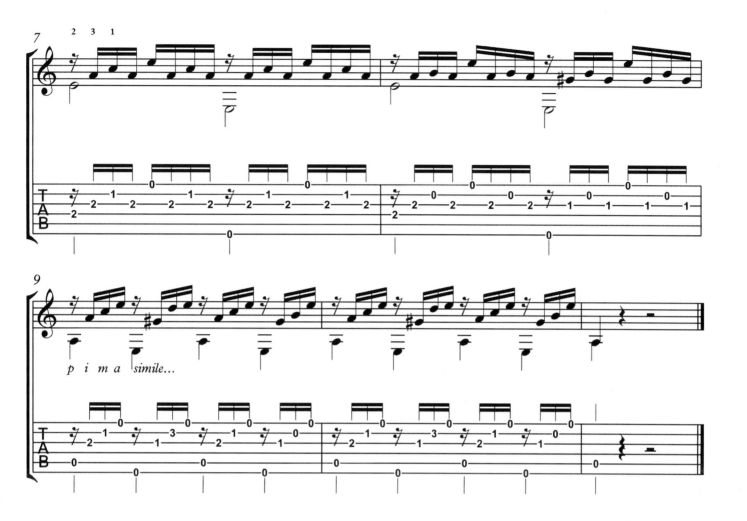

Fernando Sor's next etude also furthers the idea of arpeggiation. This etude, however, is a bit more rhythmic in nature. A rapid arpeggio is executed, followed by a note that is held.

Example 7e - Fernando Sor's Op. 60 No. 18

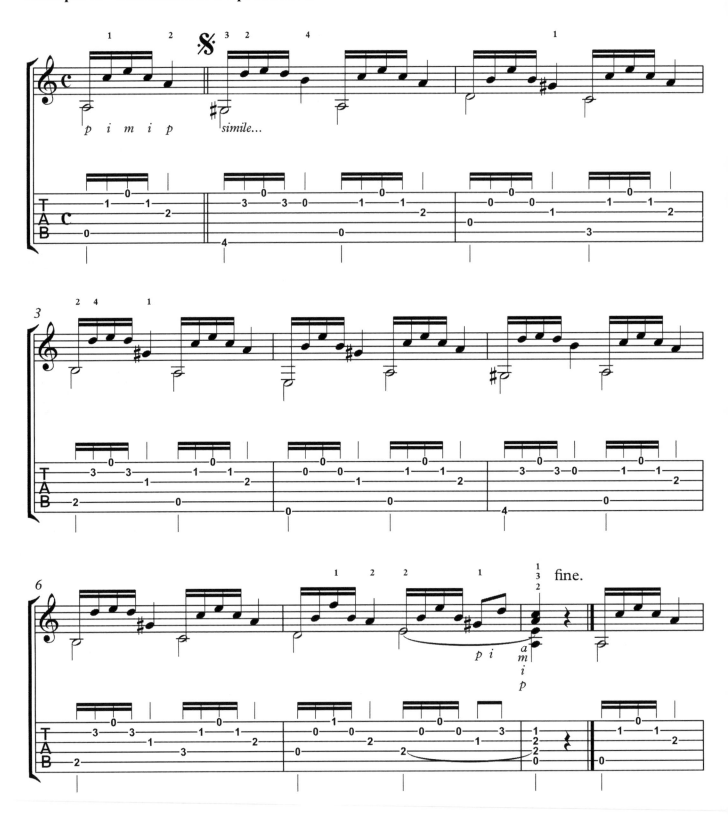

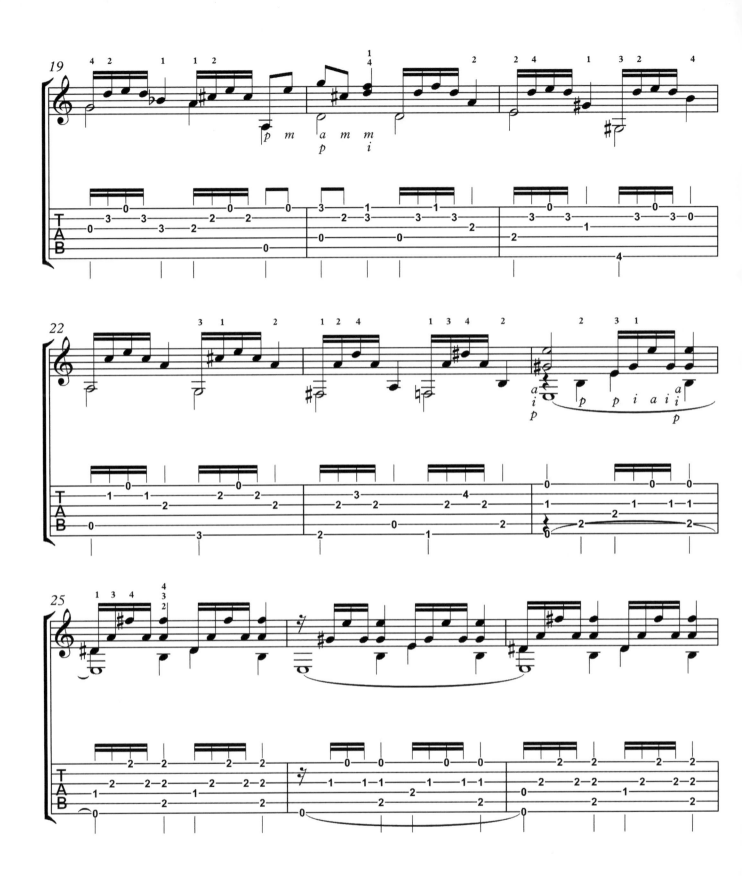

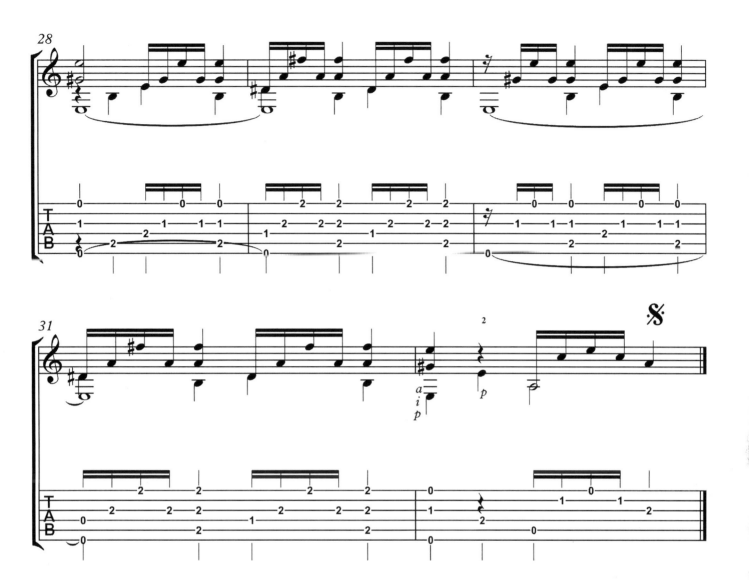

The focus of this etude is voice balancing. Be sure to make the high E-string stand out above all the rest.

Example 7f - Francisco Tárrega Etude in E Minor

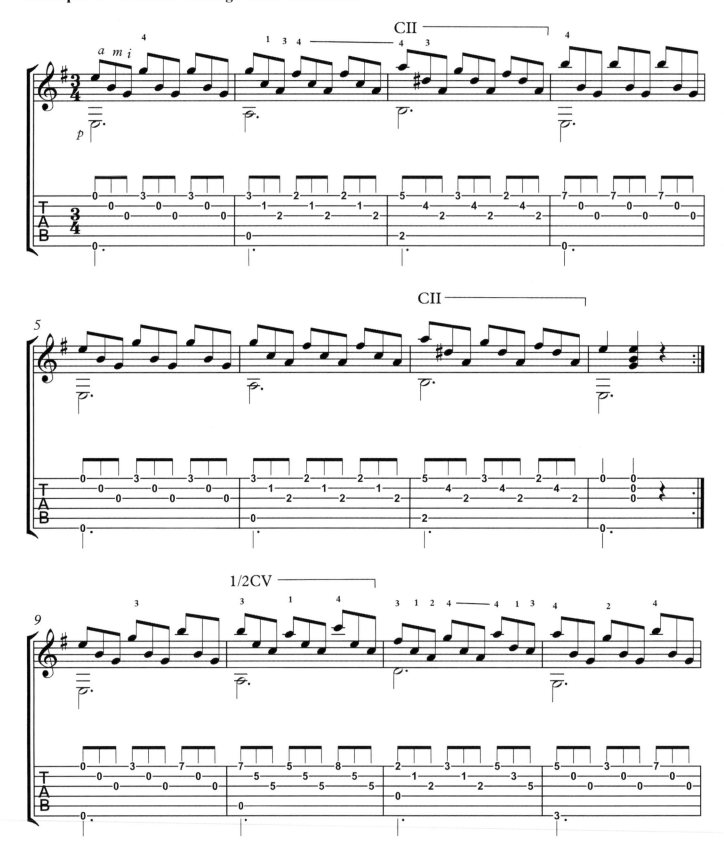

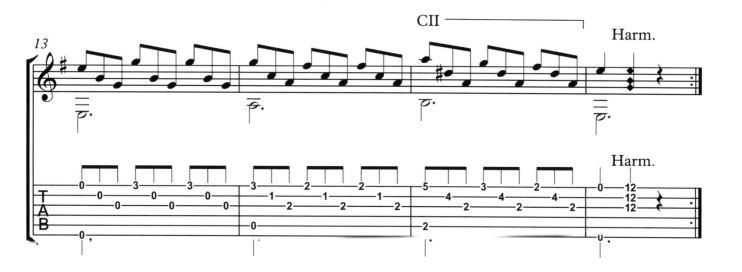

Chapter Eight – First Set of Challenging Studies

The next two arpeggios conclude examples from Mauro Giuliani's Op. 1. The entire opus consists of 120 daily studies. Any player who masters all the picking patterns from this opus is guaranteed the ability to pick through anything.

Example 8a - Mauro Giuliani Op. 1 No. 19

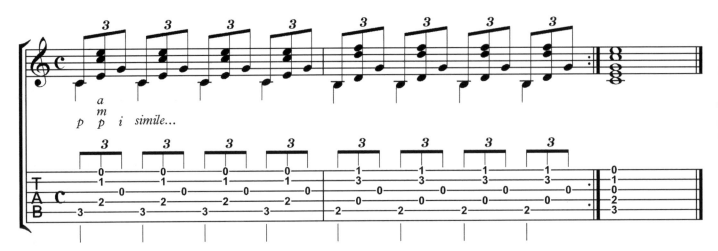

Example 8b - Mauro Giuliani Op. 1 No. 20

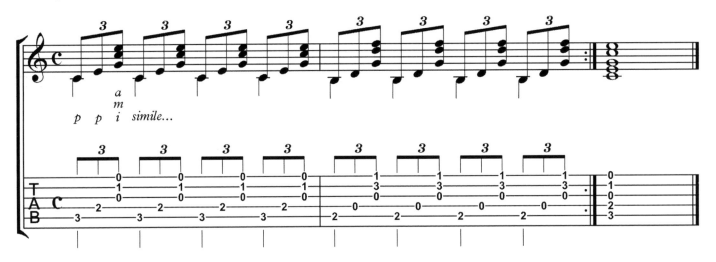

Fernando Sor's study in G Major is likely to remind you of a Beatle's tune. Its lively 6/8 rhythm pulls the player forward, and its simple melody includes great voice leading. Be sure to emphasize the beats, bringing the melody out above the accompaniment.

Example 8c – Fernando Sor Op. 60 No. 19

The next piece, Luis Milan's First Pavana, is a lovely renaissance dance. Notice the time signature is in *cut time.* In other words, it indicates to the player to *cut the note values in half.* Each whole-note is counted as a half-note, and each quarter-note is counted as an eighth note.

Example 8d – Luis Milan Pavana No. 1

Matteo Carcassi's first etude in his Op. 60 is one of the best for improving scale technique. Observe the right-hand fingerings very carefully, and practise each section slowly. This piece should be played as rapidly as possible, but that does not preclude the need to practise slowly at first.

Example 8e – Matteo Carcassi Op. 60 No. 1

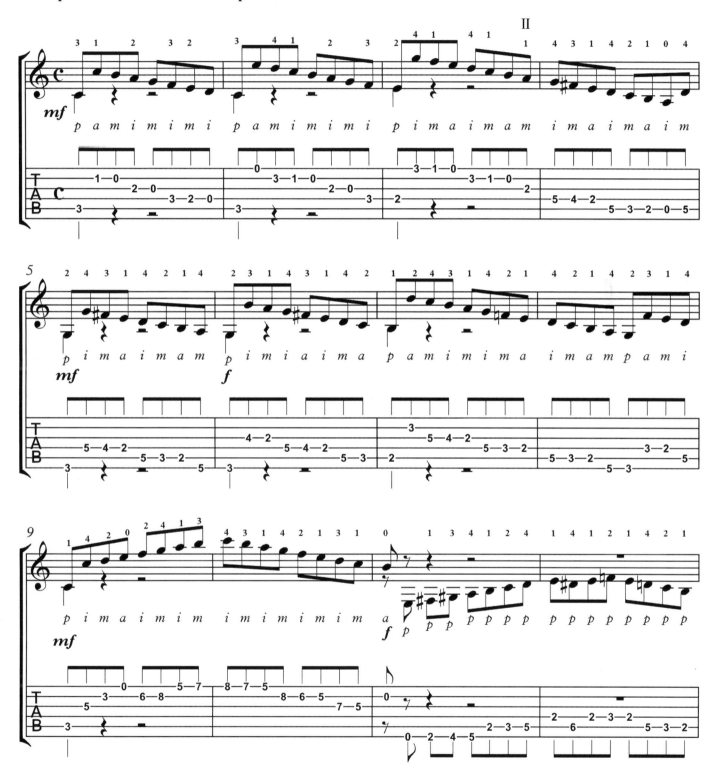

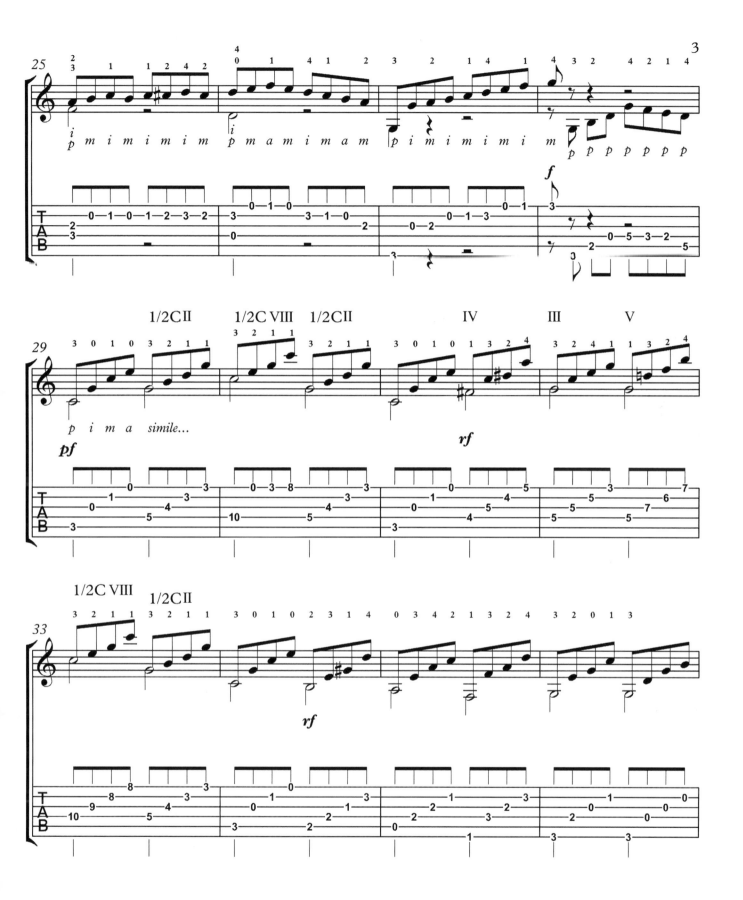

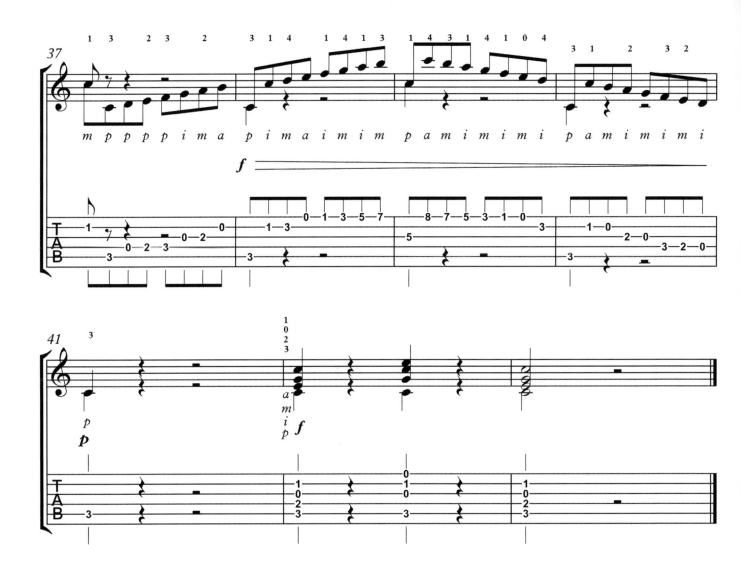

Chapter Nine – Introduction to Tremolo, and More Challenging Studies

The subject of this next etude is tremolo. Tremolo is a rapid succession of notes that give the impression of a single, sustained melody. Practise this finger pattern slowly at first, even leaving out the left-hand entirely if necessary.

Example 9a – Matteo Carcassi Op. 60 No. 2

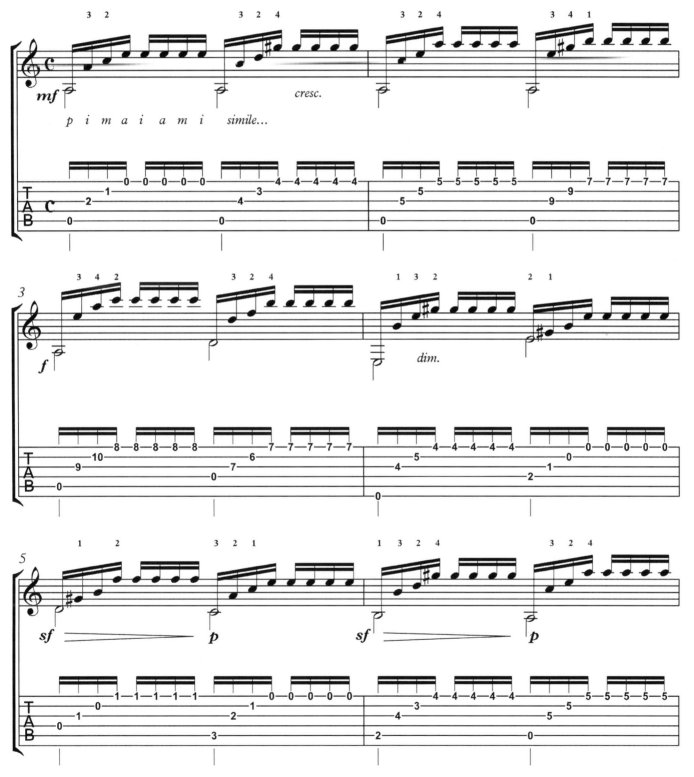

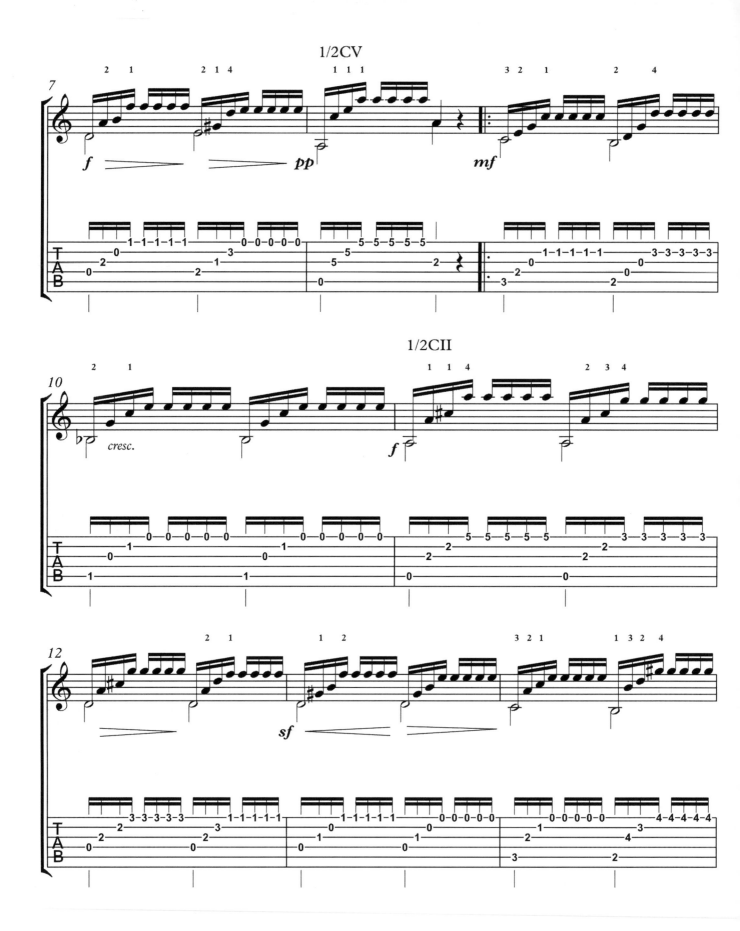

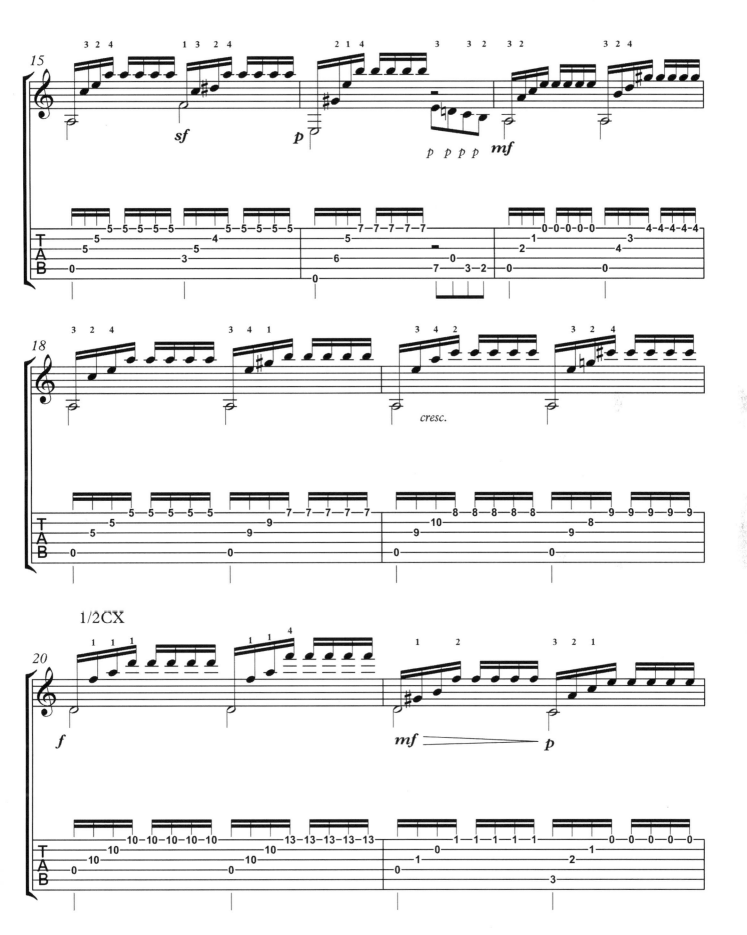

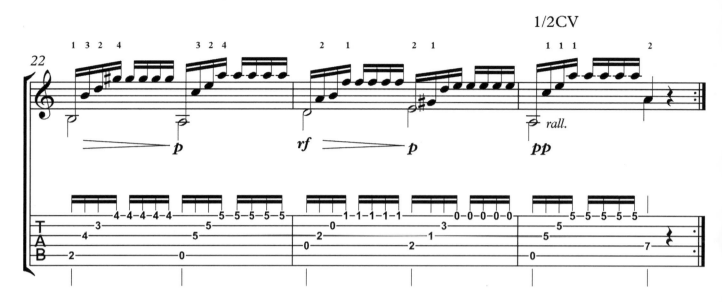

This piece is like the first of the Pavanas, but is written in the key of G Major.

Example 9b – Luis Milan Pavana No. 2

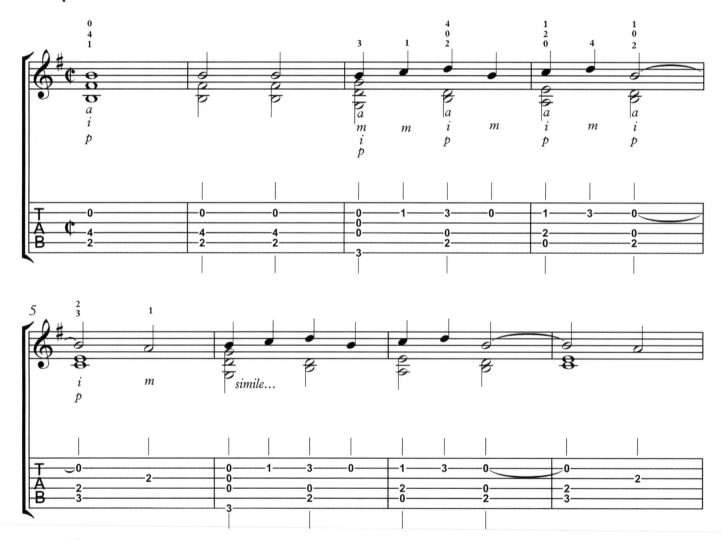

2/6CIII

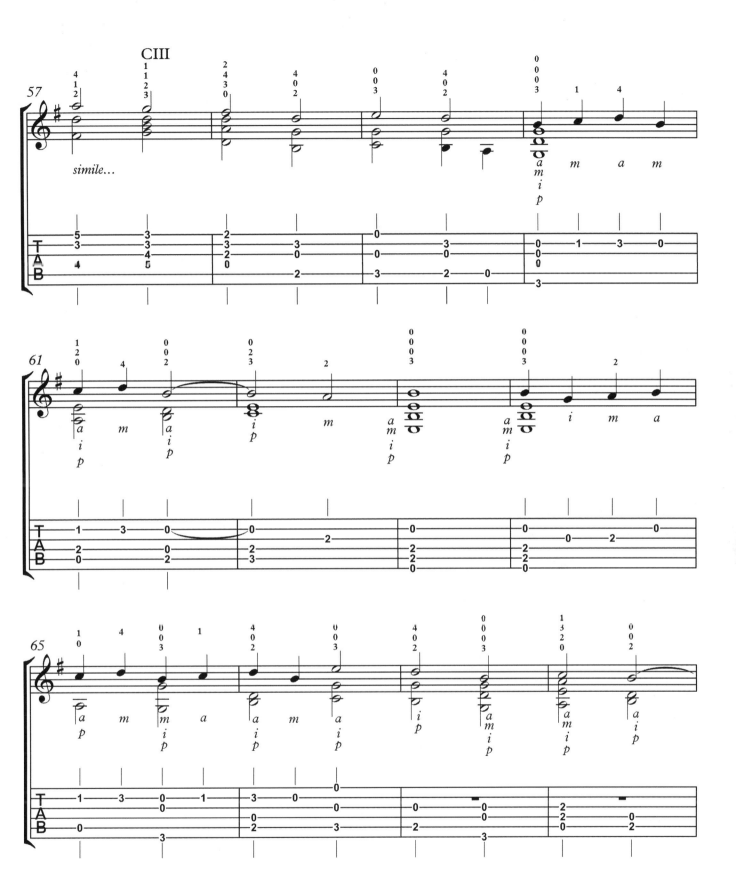

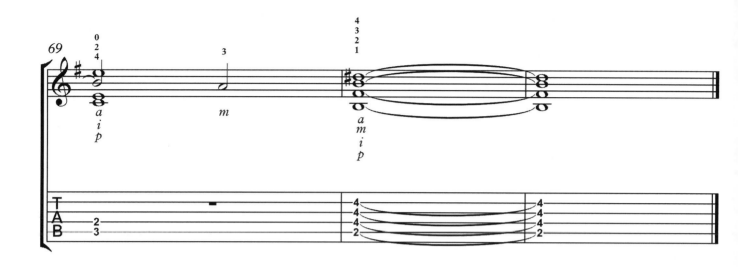

Chapter Ten – Final Studies

This etude, much like the study in E Minor by Francisco Tárrega, is all about the melody. Make the top note of each chord sing out above the rest.

Example 10a – Matteo Carcassi Op. 60 No. 3

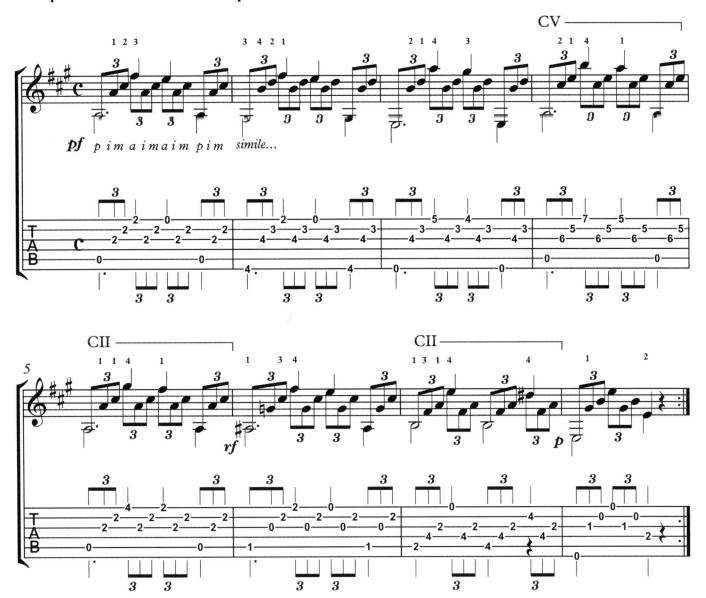

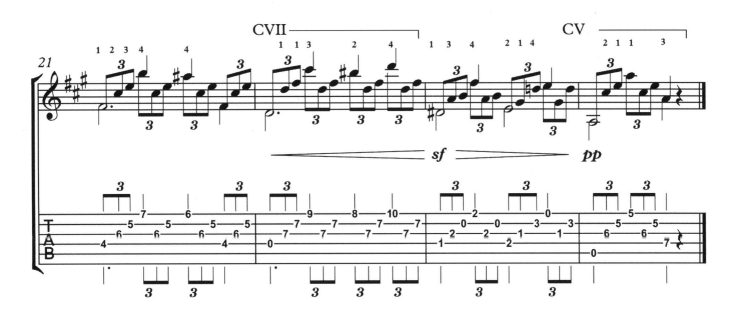

This last piece of the book is challenging and fast. The chord switches include barres, shifts and multiple voices. Practise slowly at first!

Example 10b – Luis Milan Pavana No. 3

1/2CI

simile…

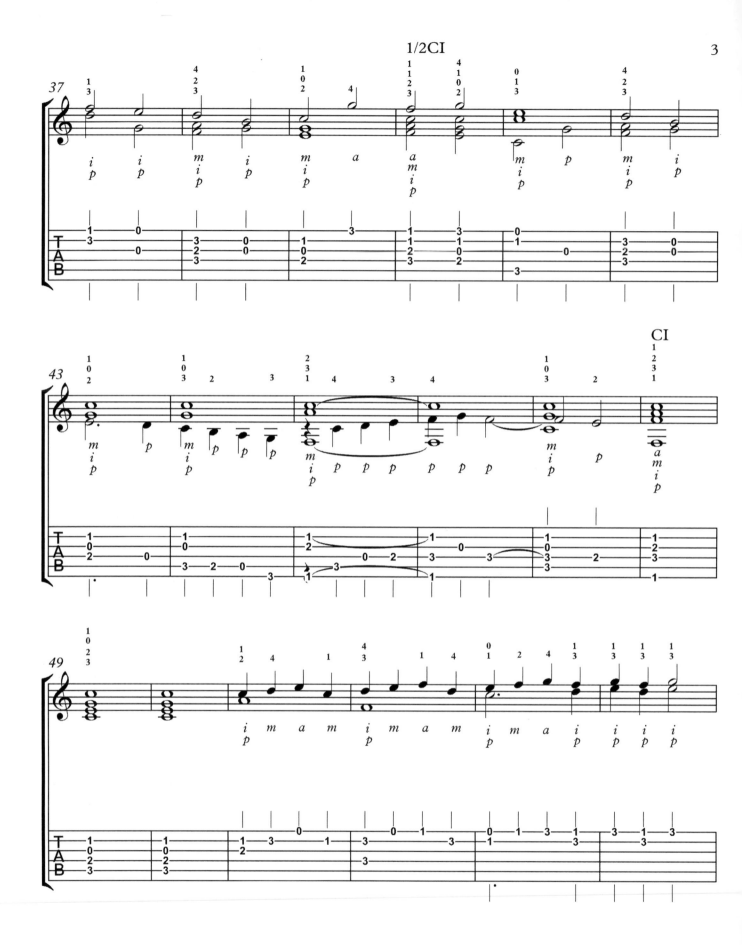

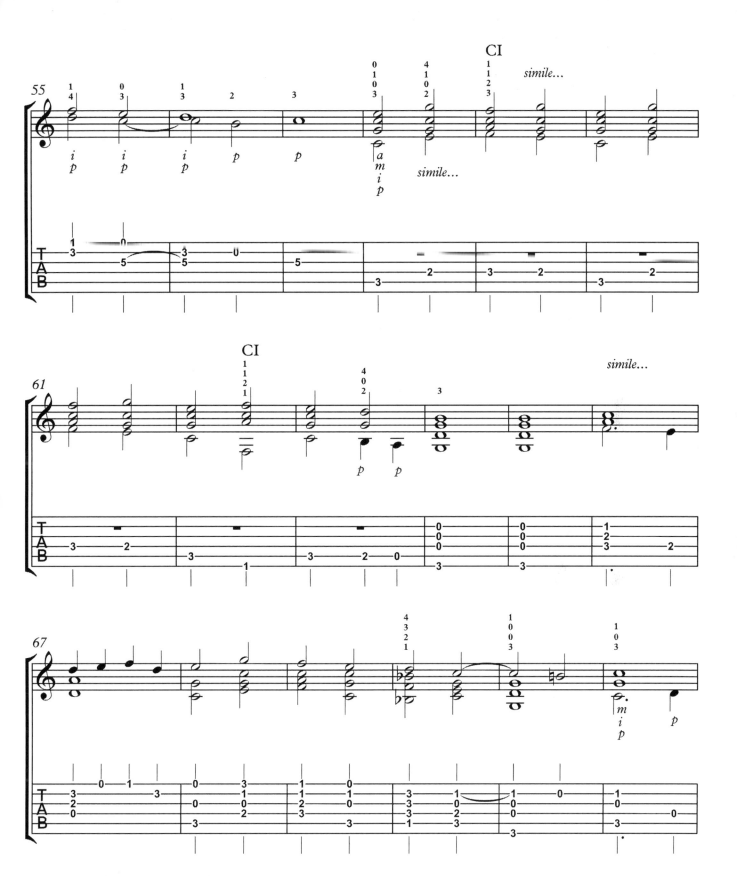

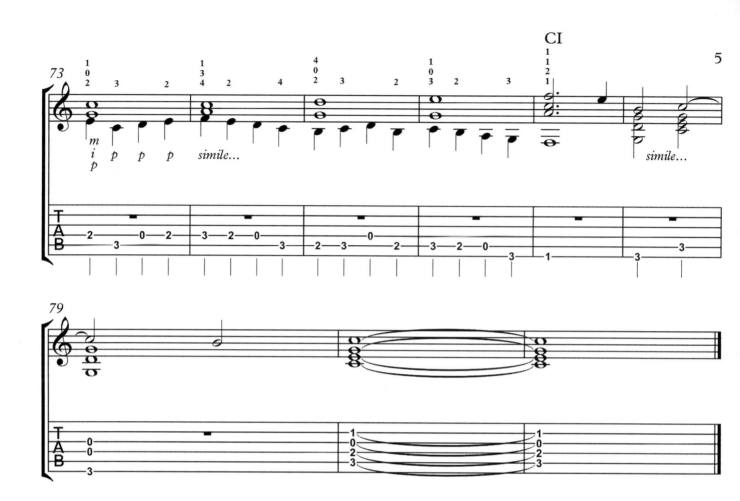

Chapter Eleven – Scales and Chords

This chapter presents a variety of chords as well as scales. Use these chords and scales to get familiar with your keys, as well as to warm up.

Example 11a – The C Major Scale

Example 11b – Chords in C Major

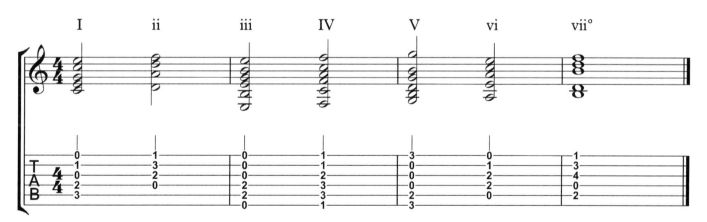

Example 11c – The G Major Scale

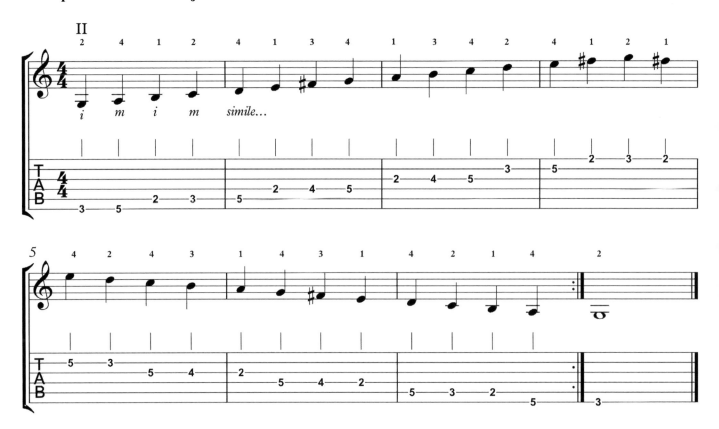

Example 11d – Chords in G Major

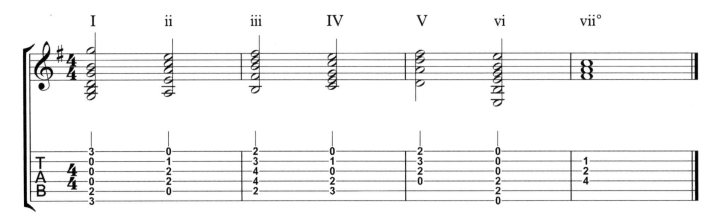

Example 11e – The D Major Scale

Example 11f – Chords in D Major

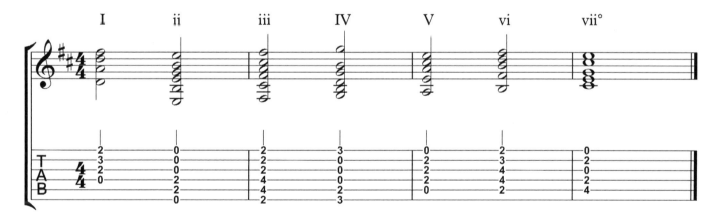

Example 11g – The A Major Scale

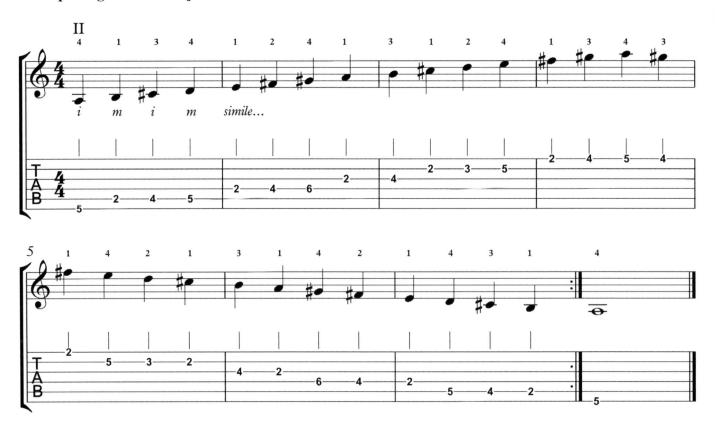

Example 11h – Chords in A Major

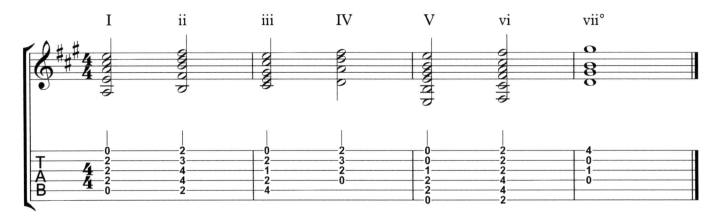

Example 11i – The E Major Scale

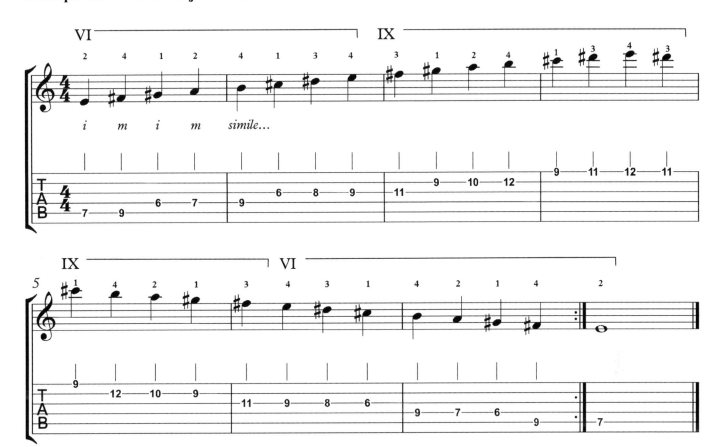

Example 11j – Chords in E Major

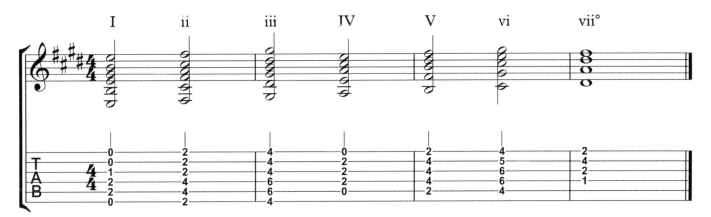

Example 11k – The F Major Scale

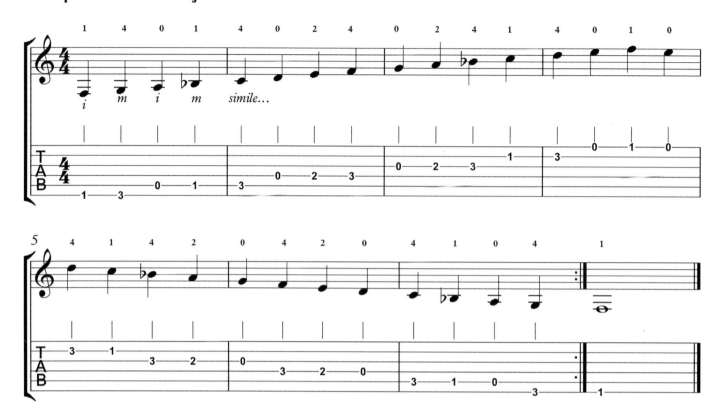

Example 11l – Chords in F Major

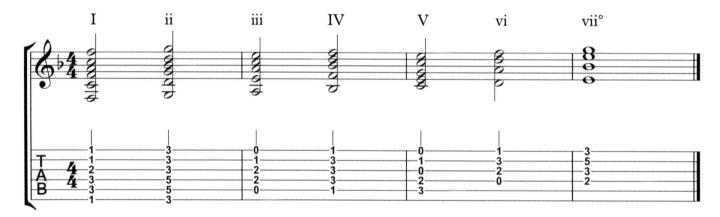

Example 11m – The A Minor Scale

Example 11n – Chords in A Minor

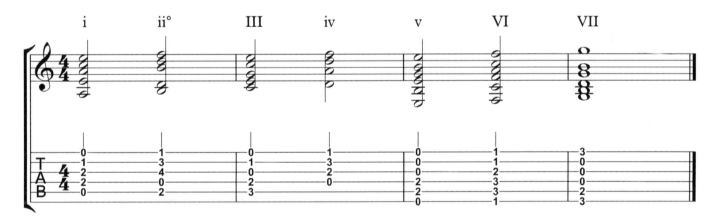

Example 11o – The E Minor Scale

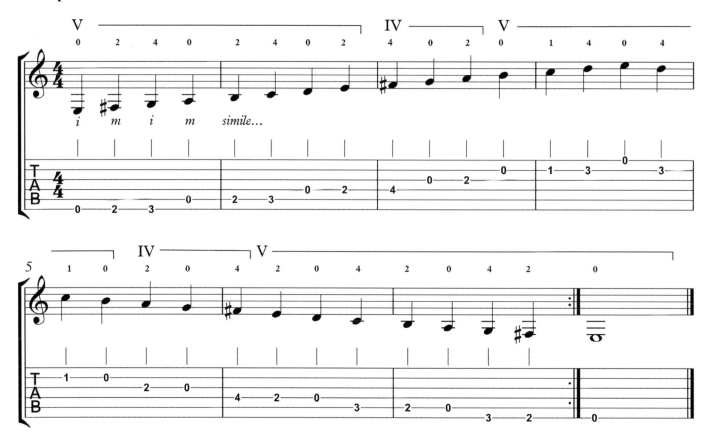

Example 11p – Chords in E Minor

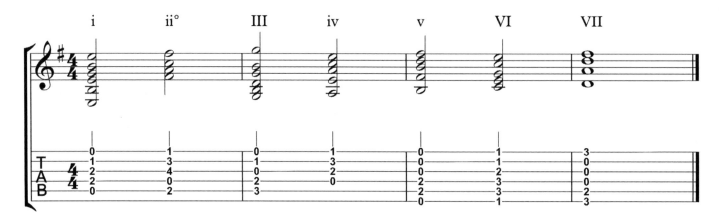

Other Books from Fundamental Changes

The Complete Guide to Playing Blues Guitar Book One: Rhythm Guitar

The Complete Guide to Playing Blues Guitar Book Two: Melodic Phrasing

The Complete Guide to Playing Blues Guitar Book Three: Beyond Pentatonics

The Complete Guide to Playing Blues Guitar Compilation

The CAGED System and 100 Licks for Blues Guitar

Minor ii V Mastery for Jazz Guitar

Jazz Blues Soloing for Guitar

Guitar Scales in Context

Guitar Chords in Context

The First 100 Chords for Guitar

Jazz Guitar Chord Mastery

Complete Technique for Modern Guitar

Funk Guitar Mastery

The Complete Technique, Theory & Scales Compilation for Guitar

Sight Reading Mastery for Guitar

Rock Guitar Un-CAGED

The Practical Guide to Modern Music Theory for Guitarists

Beginner's Guitar Lessons: The Essential Guide

Chord Tone Soloing for Jazz Guitar

Chord Tone Soloing for Bass Guitar

Voice Leading Jazz Guitar

Guitar Fretboard Fluency

The Circle of Fifths for Guitarists

First Chord Progressions for Guitar

The First 100 Jazz Chords for Guitar

100 Country Licks for Guitar

Pop & Rock Ukulele Strumming

Walking Bass for Jazz and Blues

Guitar Finger Gym

The Melodic Minor Cookbook

The Chicago Blues Guitar Method

Heavy Metal Rhythm Guitar

Heavy Metal Lead Guitar

Progressive Metal Guitar

Heavy Metal Guitar Bible

Exotic Pentatonic Soloing for Guitar

The Complete Jazz Guitar Soloing Compilation

The Jazz Guitar Chords Compilation

Fingerstyle Blues Guitar

The Complete DADGAD Guitar Method

Country Guitar for Beginners

Beginner Lead Guitar Method

The Country Fingerstyle Guitar Method

Beyond Rhythm Guitar

Rock Rhythm Guitar Playing

Fundamental Changes in Jazz Guitar

Neo-Classical Speed Strategies for Guitar

100 Classic Rock Licks for Guitar

The Beginner's Guitar Method Compilation

100 Classic Blues Licks for Guitar

The Country Guitar Method Compilation

Country Guitar Soloing Techniques

Printed in Great Britain
by Amazon